Money Smarts

A Practical Guide to Financial Independence for Young Adults

Renae C. Linde

Table of Contents

Introduction

One afternoon, as I was enjoying some quality time with my adult daughter, who was 32 at the time, I asked her this question: Of all the things you learned at home and in school to prepare you for adulthood, what was the one thing you didn't learn about that you wish you had? Her response? "I wish I would've learned about how to budget and manage money."

This hit me in my core. I thought I had covered all the basics, but at that moment I realized I neglected teaching my daughter one of the most important life skills she needed to be financially successful in life. This was my inspiration for writing this book. It is my goal to share the fundamental building blocks essential for managing money wisely so that those who need and are seeking such knowledge can acquire it in a concise and relatable manner.

In an era where financial independence is both a goal and a challenge for young adults, this book offers practical, actionable insights to help you build a solid financial foundation. I wanted this book to be a comprehensive guide that takes you through the fundamentals of income, budgeting, saving, investing, and the risks to avoid in today's complex financial landscape. Through relatable stories, straightforward examples, and clear strategies, each chapter demystifies a different aspect of financial management to ensure you are equipped for success.

Beginning with understanding income, we explore the wonderful world of diverse employment opportunities, where I introduce you to ways of earning and managing money effectively.

As you progress, you'll delve into creating and maintaining a budget that fits your lifestyle, establishing a savings strategy for future security, and understanding fundamental investment options to grow your wealth. We also take an in-depth look at how to recognize scams and how to survive financial setbacks, so you stay protected and prepared.

Whether you're just starting out with your first job or side hustle or looking to add to your financial knowledge, this book will empower you to make informed, confident decisions, paving a clear path toward financial independence and stability. Let's get started!

Chapter 1:

Understanding Income - The Building Block of Financial Stability

Earning an income is the first step toward financial stability and independence, especially as you transition into adulthood. In today's evolving economic landscape, understanding and exploring various income options like traditional employment, entrepreneurial ventures, or passive income streams, can open up pathways to a secure financial future. However, deciding which method fits your lifestyle requires reflection on your goals, skills, and personal interests. Ask yourself what you enjoy doing, how much time you can commit, and what kind of work-life balance suits you best. If you don't know what you want to do as you commit yourself to self-sufficiency, relax. A lot of young adults are in the exact same condition. Simply start by picking something. It really doesn't matter what that is when you first start out. If, after a few weeks or months this selection doesn't fit your interests or lifestyle, you learned something about what you don't want. There is no right or wrong choice when you're starting out except not taking that first step. Let's look at some of your options.

Finding the Right Employment Opportunities

Traditional Full and Part-Time Employment

Traditional employment is where you may begin earning a steady income. It offers not only regular paychecks but also potential benefits such as health insurance and retirement plans.

Starting in entry-level positions provides you valuable experience and open doors for long-term career advancement and higher salaries. It's important to view traditional employment as a foundation upon which you can build other income streams.

Choosing the traditional employment path, whether full or part-time, is the safest option for you as you start out in the workforce. Why? Because it provides you the assurance that you will have stable compensation for your work. At the same time, however, there are cons that go along with the pros: inconvenient schedules, less time with friends/family/social activities, or being assigned tasks you may find unpleasant. Consider Madison, a dedicated night school student at a local community technical college. One afternoon, while checking out at the grocery store, her credit card was repeatedly declined.

Feeling anxious, she asked the cashier to remove some items so her purchase would go through. Feeling down and embarrassed, she walked home thinking about how to make extra money while studying. In the end, Madison decided that getting a regular job at a nearby store would be the best choice. This job would help her keep track of her earnings and set realistic financial goals. She also realized that she needed a reliable used car to make it easier to get to her classes and work. With a steady work schedule and guaranteed income, she expected to buy her car within three to six months, making a regular job the best option for her situation.

Working traditional jobs not only equips students with financial stability, but it also cultivates a sense of responsibility and time management skills. This practical experience in a professional setting can prove invaluable as students transition to full-time roles in their respective fields post-graduation.

In Madison's case, her traditional retail position not only addressed her immediate financial concerns but also facilitated the development of skills necessary for future job prospects. Through interactions with customers and co-workers, she learned the importance of teamwork, communication, and problem solving, all of which are essential competencies in the workplace. Madison's experience highlights how traditional employment can bridge the gap between education and career readiness. The lessons learned in a retail environment translate into skills that are highly sought after in any industry. Traditional jobs also offer excellent networking opportunities. Working in retail lets people meet many others, like managers and customers, who can provide useful connections and references. For Madison, each interaction was a chance to get closer to her goal of working in technology. Many students, like Madison, want more than just money; they also want to improve their resumes. Traditional jobs cultivate a variety of skills and experiences, making candidates more appealing to future employers. Showing a strong work ethic and the ability to manage both work and school responsibilities shows that a candidate is ready for the workforce.

On the other hand, the commitment to traditional employment may mean sacrificing certain experiences typical of college life. Long hours spent working can lead to missed social gatherings or networking events crucial for building professional relationships. As students weigh the pros and cons of traditional jobs, it becomes essential for them to prioritize their time effectively. The key lies in striking a balance between work, study, and social engagements.

Let's examine another case: John is a full-time student navigating his second year of a business degree. He entered the realm of traditional employment by securing a part-time position as a marketing assistant at a local startup. For John, this opportunity not only provided financial relief but allowed him to apply classroom theory to real-world scenarios. He could assist with social media campaigns, helping him understand market dynamics and consumer behavior more deeply. Plus, this hands-on experience ensured that his resume stood out among his peers when he began applying for internships post-graduation.

It's important to consider the benefits tied to traditional jobs. Employers often provide additional perks such as paid time off, flexible working hours, and opportunities for professional development. These advantages can create an enriching work environment that encourages employee growth.

By being attuned to these benefits, students can maximize their employment experience, turning it into an enriching period of personal and professional growth. Ultimately, traditional employment serves as a multifaceted tool for students like Madison and John. It provides a financial lifeline while cultivating critical soft skills, networking opportunities, and practical experience. As they navigate their academic journeys, traditional jobs can lead to successful transitions into their future careers.

The journey towards achieving career goals is often fraught with financial and personal challenges, especially for students. Traditional employment provides a practical solution to these issues, ensuring steady income while offering significant opportunities for personal development. It prepares students for their transition into the workforce, equipping them with the skills necessary to thrive in their chosen professions. By viewing traditional employment as both a necessary and beneficial part of their educational experience, students can effectively set the stage for a bright and successful future.

Neighborhood Side Hustles

Starting a neighborhood side hustle is a fantastic way for young adults to earn extra income, gain work experience, and build connections within their local community. Here's a closer look at some practical ideas that are readily accessible and potentially highly rewarding.

1. Pet Services: Dog Walking and Pet Sitting

If you enjoy spending time with animals, offering pet services like dog walking or pet sitting can be a fun and flexible way to make money. Many pet owners, especially those with busy schedules or older pets, need reliable help to keep their furry friends healthy and happy. Dog walking is ideal if you love being outdoors and getting exercise while making money. You can also consider pet sitting for neighbors who go on vacation or have to work late hours. Starting is simple. Create a profile on pet service apps like Rover or Wag! or post in local neighborhood groups.

You could also print and post fliers on community bulletin boards in local grocery or convenient stores where they allow. Building a good reputation is key in this business, so ask satisfied customers to leave reviews or recommend your services to others.

2. Lawn Care and Gardening Services

Lawn care is another simple to start and maintain side hustle, especially during spring and summer when many people seek help with mowing, edging, and maintaining their lawns. This type of work doesn't require an extensive skill set—just basic knowledge of lawnmowers, trimmers, and gardening tools is often enough. Having a leaf blower or a push broom to clean up clippings is also a plus. Many potential customers, such as busy families or elderly neighbors, appreciate someone trustworthy who can take over these time-consuming and for some, physically challenging, yard tasks. In addition to regular lawn maintenance, you could offer seasonal services like raking leaves, planting flowers, or cleaning up yards after storms. Start by advertising your services through neighborhood flyers, community boards, or word-of-mouth. You can often get started with very little money up front, especially if you already have access to basic lawn care equipment.

3. Tutoring and Academic Support

Are you good at math, science, or language arts? Maybe you play an instrument and find yourself helping classmates with tips and pointers to help them play better. If this is you, maybe tutoring younger students in your neighborhood is an avenue you'd want to explore. Tutoring can be a highly rewarding way to earn extra cash while sharing your knowledge. It's flexible and can be done in person or virtually, depending on your preference and the client's needs. Parents often seek reliable and relatable young adults to help their children improve academically. You might offer support in specific subjects or general study skills, homework help, and exam preparation. In addition to school subjects, you could also offer tutoring in other areas like music, art, or even technology skills. To start, get the word out. Let neighbors and friends know about your services or create a profile on tutoring platforms. This side hustle not only generates income but also allows you as a mentor, to make a positive impact on your mentees' lives.

4. Babysitting or Childcare Services

Babysitting is another side hustle with local demand, particularly if you're experienced in looking after children. Many parents are willing to pay well for someone trustworthy who can engage their kids with activities or help with homework. Consider completing a basic first-aid or CPR course to add to your credentials, which can reassure parents. Start by offering your services to neighbors and build a strong client base through recommendations. You can also create your profile using apps like Care.com or Sittercity.

5. Delivery and Errand Services

If you have reliable transportation, offering delivery or errand services can be a helpful side hustle in your neighborhood. Many people appreciate assistance with grocery shopping, picking up prescriptions, or delivering packages, especially elderly neighbors or those with mobility issues. This side hustle allows you to offer support within your community while earning. Advertise locally, and make sure to set clear boundaries and delivery zones for your services to keep things manageable.

Starting a Side Hustle

Starting a neighborhood side hustle doesn't have to be complicated. Begin by identifying your skills and interests and think about how you can use them to meet local needs. Talk to neighbors, post on community boards, and use social media to spread the word. Good communication and reliability are essential — customers want someone they can trust.

Building these types of side hustles within your community offers several benefits: you'll meet new people, earn income, and make a positive impact. Never underestimate the power of meeting face-to-face and working directly with people in your community. You'll be amazed at all the things you learn about once you start getting to know them. With time and consistency, a neighborhood side hustle can grow into a meaningful source of income, a valuable learning experience, and perhaps even the start of a small business.

Freelancing

While traditional employment offers stability and a host of benefits, freelancing and the gig economy present exciting opportunities for those seeking flexibility. Freelance work allows you to explore diverse career paths, network, and gain practical knowledge while simultaneously building a personal brand. Whether you're writing, designing, or coding, each project adds to your skill set, making you more marketable in the long run.

To succeed, it's important for you to focus on building a strong portfolio that showcases your best work. Freelancing can be quite lucrative, especially if you're great at time management, financial management, and the practice of self-discipline. However, this great reward comes with greater risks, such as less job security and inconsistent income.

Internships and Apprenticeships

Internships and apprenticeships act as vital gateways to permanent employment and self-employment opportunities by offering hands-on, skilled experience in your chosen field. The experience gained during these programs can equip you with industry-specific knowledge and insider connections, setting you apart from your peers when applying for jobs or starting your own business. Often, the insights you gain can help refine your career goals, ensuring that your path aligns with your interests and strengths.

Valuable experience aside, internships and apprenticeships are often unpaid or low-paying, which can be challenging as you try to make ends meet. Also, there's no guarantee that, after investing all your time, there will be a job offer in the end— which may be a hard pill to swallow after investing time and effort into the position. It can even be seen as holding you back from taking the time to seek full-time employment.

Temporary Work

Temporary work strikes a balance for you as a student or someone juggling multiple commitments. These roles provide you financial independence with no long-term commitment, and they enhance your resume by helping you develop diverse skills and the ability to manage responsibilities effectively.

Temporary roles offer the chance for you to work in competitive fields and help you make informed decisions about your career preferences. One of the best things about temporary work is that agencies, depending upon the specialty and the local job market, can commonly have you placed in a paying job within a week, and frequently the next day.

On the flip side, temporary jobs are like the business equivalent to "try before you buy," only with employees. A temporary assignment could lead to a permanent job offer with the client company, but the opposite can also be true. With most agencies, the client company has the right to refuse your service with them, but you also have that same right with the client company if you find the assignment is not a good fit for you. Job insecurity, reliance on agencies, and inconsistent employment in temporary work can lead to fluctuating income and challenges in financial planning. Also, some workers face a risk of being stuck in a cycle of temporary jobs, which may hinder long-term career growth.

Passive Income: Digital Products, Affiliate Marketing, and Investments

Digital Products and Affiliate Marketing

Creating digital products offers an innovative way to generate residual income. Whether you're offering online courses, e-books, or printables, you can earn residual income long after the initial product launch. You will need some initial up-front money for things like supplies, subscriptions, learning aids and technology, but once you have created your digital product(s), they usually need very little upkeep, leaving you more time to concentrate on adding to your collection or trying out new projects.

Affiliate marketing taps into the power of social media, enabling you to earn commissions by promoting other people's products while building a platform (or audience) on your social media. Affiliate marketing is attractive because if you can organically hone your niche, it's easier to make your affiliate efforts more authentic. Authenticity increases the likelihood of success as well.

Once you've paved your lane (niche); will it glitter? Getting likes and followers is one thing, converting them into buyers for your products is quite another. If you promote and market yourself well, you can maximize your revenue. The digital market is highly competitive and saturated, and you might find it hard to stand out. In addition, there's the risk of dealing with intellectual property theft or copyright infringement. As such, going digital requires a lot of time and effort with no guaranteed return.

Investments

Making money off money that you have set aside is an avenue that is becoming more attractive to young people today. Whether you're selling things online or investing in stocks and Exchange-Traded Funds (ETFs), passive income often requires minimal active involvement once it's set up (provided you spent sufficient time and effort doing your due diligence and researching various options). Investing early and wisely can yield returns over time, contributing to your wealth accumulation and financial security. Understanding the stock market might seem daunting at first, but many resources and apps are available to simplify the process, making it accessible to you as a beginner.

Inherent market risks, such as the potential loss of your principal or initial investment, can be a deterrent. Please note that there's no guarantee of positive returns, and ill-informed decisions can be costly when dealing with volatile short-term markets. We'll dive deeper into investments in a later chapter.

Balancing Multiple Income Sources

When you are pursuing financial growth, diversifying income streams plays an essential role. Instead of relying on a single source of income, you can have multiple avenues to dramatically reduce your financial risk. Whether you're facing an economic downturn or dealing with unexpected personal circumstances, diversified income acts as a cushion, allowing you more control over your financial choices. Diversification is not just about mitigating risks; it's also about expanding opportunities. An essential part of diversifying income is staying adaptable.

Financial tracking techniques like budgeting and tax preparation come in handy to simplify tasks. Using digital tools, such as budgeting apps or spreadsheets, can help you monitor your cash flow from various sources.

These tools allow you to categorize your income and expenses, giving you a clear picture of where your money is coming from and how it's being spent. With all that you are investing, it becomes all the more important to have tracking mechanisms and a backup plan to protect yourself in the event of unforeseen circumstances.

Here's an example of diversification at work. To diversify his income, 27-year-old graphic designer Thayer started an online store to sell his artwork while continuing to work full time. In the beginning, the varying demands of keeping his new customers happy overwhelmed him and his work schedule.

Thayer often stayed up late and pulled all-nighters, thus neglecting his health and social life. Thayer was determined to avoid burnout and make things work, so he implemented several time management strategies. One such strategy allowed him to prioritize and focus his energy on orders that were important. Also, he created a weekly schedule that allocated specific time blocks to managing his online store and performing other freelance work.

Next, Thayer focused on self-care. He blocked off nonnegotiable time for exercise and other forms of downtime. The Swiss Cheese Method, a productivity technique where you break down large tasks into smaller, more manageable chunks, creating "holes" in the task that can be worked on over time inspired him to break down tasks; this method helped him reduce procrastination and increase productivity.

Lastly, Thayer downloaded a budgeting app to track his income and expenses, as well as to review and adapt his income strategies regularly. This strategy allowed him to remain flexible enough to navigate during slower periods. After about four months, Thayer experienced a 37% increase in online and freelance income. And, to his delight, he felt less stressed and more in control of his time and money.

The Sum of Our Parts: Key Takeaways

In this chapter, we explored the foundations of earning income and the different avenues that can set you on a path to financial stability. From understanding traditional employment to exploring side hustles, freelancing, and passive income, each method offers unique benefits that contribute to a diversified financial landscape. Traditional employment provides steady income and benefits, laying a stable foundation for future ventures. Meanwhile, side hustles and freelancing introduce flexibility and growth opportunities, allowing you to capitalize on your skills and passions.

The examples of Madison and John highlighted how even entry-level positions can foster essential skills like communication, teamwork, and time management, which are invaluable in any career. Balancing multiple income streams also reduces financial risk, preparing you for life's unpredictable moments. Ultimately, achieving financial stability is about finding the right combination of income sources that align with your skills, interests, and lifestyle. By understanding these income options and thoughtfully incorporating them into your life, you'll be better equipped to navigate your financial journey confidently. Now, equipped with this knowledge, take the first steps to secure a future where financial independence is within reach.

Chapter 2:

Demystifying Expenses - Needs vs. Wants

NEEDS
— FOOD —

WANTS
— ENTERTAINMENT —

Welcome to understanding the difference between needs and wants. It's a journey of separating what is essential for daily living from those things that simply bring pleasure, yet aren't necessary. Let's take a critical look at spending habits, dissecting how to determine whether they fit the mold of need or want. Such reflection will create room to allow priorities that truly matter, and it will help one develop a stronger sense of financial autonomy, paving the way for a more balanced and fulfilling economic existence. What are practical strategies for effectively categorizing daily expenses? After celebrating her 29th birthday, Hannah embarked on a new chapter by moving into her own apartment. However, within three months, she grappled with the reality of mounting bills. Previously accustomed to relying on her parents for financial support, she hesitated to reach out after learning that her father had recently lost his job. Faced with uncertainty, Hannah pondered what steps she could take to regain control of her financial situation.

Hannah first realized she was spending too much on things like eating out, rideshares, clothes, and fun activities. These extra costs were too much for her budget and were taking away money from important bills like rent, phone services, utilities, and insurance. Wanting to fix this problem, she made a spreadsheet to track her spending each month. Her goal was simple: to redefine her financial priorities while gaining a comprehensive understanding of her expenditures. To visually illustrate her spending patterns, Hannah realized she needed to identify her missteps. Armed with her spreadsheet, she compared her fixed costs to her variable expenses.

This analysis was a turning point, as it enabled her to embrace budgeting as a tangible practice, through which she could allocate funds to cover essential fixed costs while establishing realistic limits on her discretionary spending. Adopting a structured framework known as the 50/30/20 rule, Hannah allocated 50% of her income towards necessities, set 30% towards personal desires, and reserved the remaining 20% for savings and debt repayment. Over nine months, Hannah learned a lot about her finances. Although she still spent too much on things that varied from month to month, she was proud that she had kept her fixed costs under control for the last three months. This new skill helped her feel more at ease and less stressed. To further illustrate the impact of Hannah's journey, consider

Mark's story. Mark, like Hannah, moved into his own space after graduating from college.

However, with a limited income from his entry-level job, he quickly found himself overwhelmed by bills and debt. Initially, he too sought comfort in immediate gratification, such as spontaneous nights out with friends or online shopping sprees. Recognizing the need for change, Mark established a strict budget, meticulously tracking his income and expenses through various budgeting apps. He implemented the 80/20 rule, directing 80% of his income towards essential costs and allowing himself only 20% for discretionary spending. This decisive shift not only helped him manage his living expenses but also carved a path towards building savings and paying off debt.

Through their shared experiences, both Hannah and Mark discovered valuable financial principles. The act of creating budgets transformed their financial lives, enabling them to cultivate prudence in managing expenses and fostering a mindset of financial independence. This careful plan also affected other parts of their lives. Hannah learned to cook at home, which lowered her food costs while allowing her to enjoy making meals. Mark started seeking out free local events for fun, which improved his social life without costing much. As they continued their money-management journeys, they saw that budgeting was more than just a task; it was a way to gain control. Hannah and Mark agreed that understanding finances was an important skill, giving them power over their money choices and future goals.

Hannah and Mark's stories show how important it is to look at spending habits and set new financial goals. Their experiences highlight how people try to manage adult life in a world focused on consumerism. By taking charge of their money, they not only found their independence but also became supporters of others in similar situations. In short, Hannah and Mark remind us that facing our financial problems honestly can lead to real change. By using good budgeting methods, understanding where the money goes, and making thoughtful choices, anyone can build a better relationship with their finances. Their paths show that, even when difficulties come up with the right attitude and tools, reaching financial stability is achievable and worth the effort.

Understanding Expenses: Fixed vs. Variable

At this point, let's explore fixed and variable expenses in more detail. Fixed expenses are those recurring costs that remain consistent from month to month. Common examples include rent, mortgage payments, insurance premiums, and loan payments. These expenses provide a stable financial baseline you can rely on when planning your monthly budget. Make it a priority to cover these essential bills without fail every time, since they are predictable and usually necessary commitments.

By identifying and budgeting for fixed expenses, you can avoid unpleasant surprises at the end of the month. Variable expenses present a distinct challenge. Unlike their fixed counterparts, these expenses fluctuate based on usage and personal choices. Groceries, dining out, entertainment, and clothing fall into this category. Because these expenses can vary, they require a bit more oversight to manage one's budget.

The unpredictability of variable expenses can make budgeting seem like an exercise in futility. However, adaptability is your friend. Start by tracking your spending habits for a minimum of six to eight months. Take advantage of budgeting apps, spreadsheets, or old-fashioned pen and paper. Adjusting variable expenses can lead to better savings and financial agility. Since these costs are not set in stone, they offer you room to maneuver.

Consider cooking meals at home, using a free app to watch movies, having a games night at home instead of going out, or watching the game at home with friends instead of at the bar. Small shifts in how one approaches variable expenses can have a meaningful impact on their overall budget.

For variable expenses, it's about building awareness and making conscious choices. Review past spending patterns and identify areas where small tweaks could lead to significant savings. The goal here is to maintain a balance—that is, enjoying life while staying within financial limits. Creating an emergency fund is another strategic move when managing both fixed and variable expenses. Aim to save up a minimum of six months' worth of living expenses.

To sum up, remember that facing financial challenges head-on is empowering and, more importantly, what financial literacy and independence are all about.

Responsible Credit Use and Credit Reports

Before rushing into applying for that incredible credit card offer you just got in the mail, stop a minute to read the fine print. The devil is in the details, and using credit responsibly is key to building a strong financial foundation. Although credit cards offer convenience and allow you to make purchases quickly, they can also lead to financial trouble if not used wisely. First, consider whether that gadget you have your eye on is a need or a want.

Ask yourself if there are alternative methods to acquire it like setting aside savings or putting the item on lay-away. How badly do need or want the item, and when must you have it? All these questions are relevant when making the decision to make a purchase on credit. Once you decide to take that leap, here are some strategies to ensure responsible credit use, along with examples illustrating how each approach can positively impact your financial future.

Understand and Prioritize Timely Payments

One of the most important factors in building a strong credit score is making timely payments. Every late payment can significantly impact your credit score and make it harder to secure favorable interest rates in the future. Set reminders or automate payments to help stay on track.

Example: Dottie has a credit card with a $500 balance. She makes it a priority to pay her bill in full every month. By setting up automatic payments, Dottie never misses a due date, which strengthens her credit score and avoids late fees. This habit has helped her to maintain a high credit score, putting her in a good position when she applies for a car loan with a low interest rate.

Keep Your Credit Utilization Low

Credit utilization refers to the amount of available credit you're using compared to your credit limit. A general rule of thumb is to keep your balance below 30% of your total credit limit, which shows lenders you can handle credit responsibly. If you have more than one revolving credit account, maintain this threshold for each of your accounts.

Example: Eddie has a credit card with a $1,000 limit. To keep his credit utilization low, he ensures his balance never exceeds

$300. By monitoring his spending and paying down his balance consistently, Eddie keeps his utilization within the ideal range.

His credit score improves over time, helping him qualify for better loan terms when he needs financing for a home.

Avoid Unnecessary Credit Accounts

While it can be tempting to open multiple credit cards or accounts for rewards, doing so within a short time frame can make you appear risky to lenders. Each time a lender runs a credit inquiry, it impacts your credit score, so be selective about applying for new credit.

Example: Lisa receives several credit card offers in the mail, each offering different rewards. Rather than opening multiple accounts, she chooses the one that best fits her lifestyle and avoids opening others. By doing so, Lisa builds credit with one account, avoiding the risk of debt accumulation or damaging her credit score from multiple hard inquiries.

Understand Interest Rates and Pay Off Balances in Full When Possible

Carrying a balance from month to month can lead to high interest charges, especially if your card has a high Annual Percentage Rate (APR). Try not to get into the habit of just paying the minimum amount due each month. If you do, depending on your balance and APR, you could spend decades paying off the debt and you could end up paying hundreds or even thousands of dollars in interest alone. Paying off your balance in full each month can help you avoid interest altogether and keep your debt manageable.

Example: Jerome buys a laptop with his credit card, planning to pay off the $600 balance over the next six months. After calculating the interest he would accrue ($40.89 interest with fixed payments of $106.81), he decides to save more each month to pay off the balance sooner. This saves him on interest and keeps his debt under control.

Monitor Your Credit Regularly

Regularly checking your credit report helps you stay aware of any potential errors or fraudulent activities. You're entitled to one free credit report annually from each of the three major credit bureaus, and keeping track of your report ensures that you're aware of any issues that could impact your score.

Example: Tina reviews her credit report and notices an unfamiliar account. She contacts the credit bureau and finds out her information was used fraudulently. By catching this early, Tina can dispute the charge and prevent it from affecting her credit score long-term.

Consider the Long-Term Benefits of Good Credit

Responsible credit use not only impacts your ability to borrow but can also play a role in job applications, rental agreements, and insurance premiums. Maintaining a good credit score provides flexibility in securing lower interest rates and better financial terms in the future.

Example: Isaiah is applying for an apartment in a competitive area. The landlord reviews applicants' credit histories to assess reliability. Because of Isaiah's strong credit score and history of timely payments, he was selected for the lease over other applicants. This demonstrates how responsible credit use can affect areas beyond loans and credit cards.

Building and maintaining good credit is a gradual process that pays off significantly in the long run. By prioritizing timely payments, managing credit usage, avoiding unnecessary accounts, understanding interest rates, monitoring your credit, and considering the broader impact of credit on your life, you can set a strong foundation for financial stability.

These habits not only improve your credit score but also open doors to better opportunities and reduced financial stress. Responsible credit use, practiced early and consistently, lays the groundwork for a prosperous financial future.

What is a Credit Score and How Does It Work?

A credit score is a numerical representation of your creditworthiness, indicating the likelihood that you will repay borrowed money and make timely payments. It typically ranges from 300 to 850, with higher scores representing a better credit history and lower risk to lenders.

Credit scores are determined using the information found in your credit report, which is maintained by credit bureaus such as Equifax, Experian, and TransUnion. These reports track your borrowing history, including details such as loans, credit cards, payment history, and outstanding debts. Here are the key components of a credit score:

1. Payment History (35%): The most important factor. Consistently paying your bills on time helps boost your score. Late payments, defaults, or bankruptcies can significantly lower your score.
2. Credit Utilization (30%): This is the ratio of your current credit card balances to your total credit limits. Keeping your utilization below 30% is generally beneficial for your score.
3. Length of Credit History (15%): The longer your credit history, the better. This considers the age of your oldest account, the age of your newest account, and the average age of all accounts.
4. Credit Mix (10%): Having a mix of different types of credit (credit cards, auto loans, mortgages, etc.) shows

lenders you can manage different types of debt responsibly.

5. New Credit Inquiries (10%): Applying for new credit results in a hard inquiry, which can temporarily lower your score. However, the impact is typically small and short-lived.

Why do credit scores matter? If you ever want to borrow money, banks and other lenders will check and use your credit score to determine whether to approve you for loans, credit cards, and other financial products. Higher scores often qualify you for better interest rates. Maybe you're looking for a place to live. Landlords may check your score to decide whether to rent to you. In some regions, insurance companies may use credit scores to determine how much you will pay in premiums for car or homeowner's insurance. Even certain employers may check a modified version of your credit report (not the score itself) as part of the hiring process.

Understanding your credit score and how it works can help you make better financial decisions, leading to more favorable lending terms and better financial opportunities over time.

Prioritizing and Evaluating Spending Habits

When navigating financial independence, young adults often face the challenge of distinguishing between essential and non-essential expenses. Note that necessities are expenditures needed for living and maintaining an acceptable quality of life.

Recognizing this distinction helps you effectively budget your resources and achieve your personal financial goals.

Creating a spending hierarchy is an effective strategy to further refine the management of finances. A spending hierarchy helps make informed decisions about where to allocate funds, especially when financial resources are limited. While rent and groceries should top the list, phone bills and fitness may be in the middle; they could also be lower on the list with entertainment and dining out. Having and maintaining a structured approach not only supports more disciplined spending habits; it also empowers individuals to make conscious decisions aligned with their financial goals.

Discretionary expenses are those that are unnecessary for basic survival, such as hobbies, clothing, vacations, and entertainment. Monitoring and reviewing discretionary expenditures helps individuals gain insight into their spending patterns. By identifying trends and patterns, individuals can adjust their spending to align with their financial objectives, ultimately leading to improved savings.

Reflecting on how spending aligns with personal values is yet another essential aspect of managing finances effectively. Aligning expenditures with personal priorities ensures that financial decisions contribute positively to overall life satisfaction. Take, for example, someone who values personal growth and learning. They may choose to invest in courses or educational materials rather than spend money on transient pleasures. Reflecting on spending choices allows individuals to ensure their purchases are meaningful. It reduces buyer's remorse, fostering a more purposeful approach to financial management.

It's important to reassess priorities regularly, as needs and values can change. Life changes, such as beginning a new job or moving to a new city, may shift which expenses are necessary and which ones are discretionary. Periodic reassessments and ongoing evaluations create avenues for more flexibility within a budget, allowing for adjustments that accommodate life's unpredictable nature.

By taking stock of what truly matters regularly, individuals can better align their financial decisions with their core values. They become more satisfied as personal principles resonate with lifestyle choices.

The Sum of Our Parts: Key Takeaways

In this chapter we discovered the importance of understanding financial needs versus wants. By learning to differentiate essential expenses from discretionary ones, you will be able to gain financial autonomy, prioritize essential bills, and create a balanced approach to spending. Using practical examples like Hannah and Mark's stories, we see how budgeting strategies such as the 50/30/20 rule can help transform spending habits.

Through tracking their expenses, both discovered how to manage fixed and variable costs effectively, build savings, and make more intentional choices that align with their financial goals.

We discussed the concept of budgeting for fixed expenses—such as rent and insurance—while maintaining flexibility in managing variable costs, like dining out or entertainment. Both Hannah and Mark realized how small adjustments in variable spending could make a meaningful difference, highlighting the power of adaptability and mindful budgeting.

Additionally, responsible credit use was emphasized as a vital tool for building financial stability. Establishing good habits like timely payments and maintaining low credit utilization sets a strong foundation for the future. By fostering financial literacy through budgeting and disciplined credit use, you can work toward a secure and fulfilling financial life that is aligned with your goals.

Chapter 3:

Budgeting Basics - Your Financial Road Map

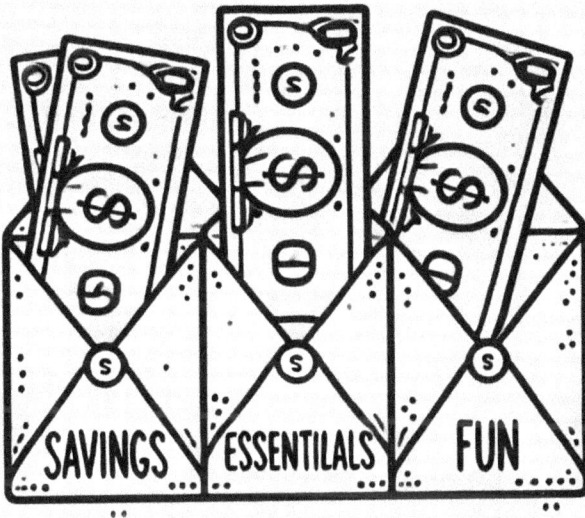

Would you take a road trip somewhere new without a GPS? I suppose you could and take the risk of getting lost. Successful money management is the trip we're taking now. What tools can you use as your financial GPS to ensure you embark down the right path?

As we begin to answer this question, let's take a moment to understand that budgeting is assigning a job to every dollar of your income. It's a forward-thinking approach to managing your finances where you deliberately allot money into a variety of categories such as savings, investments, and expenses BEFORE you spend it. Why? This ensures that every dollar has a purpose, prevents 'unintentional' spending, and aligns spending with your priorities.

Yes, I feel your eyes rolling already. But seriously, it's really not that bad. Let's begin with the fundamental principles. The goal is to turn the concept of budgeting into a powerful tool that offers freedom through structure. Read on, as this chapter will unveil the essential steps to demystify budgeting.

These days, budgeting has been made easier through the many tools readily available. These tools transform budgeting from a task into a habit. Digital apps have revolutionized how we deal with money, offering convenience and adaptability to fit various lifestyles and preferences. You'll learn about the strengths and features of tools like YNAB (You Need A Budget) and PocketGuard, and you'll gain insights into choosing the right one for you. Also, we'll review traditional methods, such as the envelope system. We discuss the importance of flexibility in budgeting, ensuring your financial strategy matures with you. Your goal is to implement effective budgeting strategies.

Budgeting ABCs: Getting Started

Budgeting methods that foster savings enhance your ability to maintain financial stability. They require a combination of tangible planning and creative approaches to adapt to changing circumstances. Flexibility is key to maintaining effective financial management as life circumstances change.

Among various methods, the traditional envelope budgeting system is a powerful tool because its approach is rooted in the tactile feeling of physically handling money. Perhaps, when you were younger, you had a piggy bank full of coins that you were saving for a special occasion. Studies have shown that physically handling cash can lead to reduced spending. On average, people spend around $20 dollars in cash, while digitally, they would spend a little over $100. Traditionally, this method involves physically dividing your budget into specific spending categories, each represented by an envelope filled with cash intended for that purpose. When the envelope is empty, it means you can no longer spend money in that category until it's replenished the following month.

Creating a budget is a powerful tool for taking control of personal finances, managing spending, and achieving financial goals. The process begins with understanding both income and expenses and applying a structured approach to balance them effectively.

Start by identifying all sources of monthly income, including your salary, freelance work, or any additional earnings. Accurately listing income provides a clear picture of what you have available to allocate each month. According to the Consumer Financial Protection Bureau, understanding your income stream is a fundamental step in building a realistic budget (CFPB, 2023). Once income is established, categorize your expenses into two main groups: fixed and variable. Fixed expenses, like rent, utilities, and insurance, are consistent monthly costs. Variable expenses, such as groceries, dining out, and entertainment, fluctuate and can often be adjusted to save money. This separation helps identify necessary versus discretionary spending, making it easier to prioritize essentials while finding areas to cut back if needed.

After listing all income and expenses, subtract total expenses from your income to determine what's left. If you're overspending, it may be necessary to adjust variable expenses or rethink some fixed costs. If there's a surplus, it can be directed toward savings or debt reduction. A popular budgeting approach is the 50/30/20 rule, developed by Elizabeth Warren and Amelia Warren Tyagi in All Your Worth. This approach suggests that you allocate 50% of your income to needs (essential costs like rent and utilities), 30% to wants (entertainment, dining out), and the remaining 20% to savings or debt repayment. For instance, if you earn $3,000 per month, aim to allocate $1,500 to needs, $900 to wants, and $600 to savings or debt. This approach provides a balanced framework that ensures financial security while allowing room for discretionary spending. Consider the following sample budget, based on the 50/30/20 rule.

Category	Item Description	Amount ($)	Frequency	Type
Income				
Salary	Monthly paycheck	$ 2,000.00	Monthly	Income
Side Job	Freelance work	$ 300.00	Monthly	Income
Investments	Dividends (converted)	$ 50.00	Monthly	Income
Bonus	Year-end performance (converted)	$ 50.00	Monthly	Income
Gifts	Cash gifts from family	$ 100.00	Monthly	Income
Income Subtotal		**$ 2,500.00**		
Expenses				
Rent/Mortgage	Housing	$ 850.00	Monthly	Fixed
Car Payment	Loan	$ 300.00	Monthly	Fixed
Car Insurance	Insurance	$ 100.00	Monthly	Fixed
Fixed Expenses Subtotal		**$ 1,250.00**		
Groceries	Food supplies	$ 350.00	Monthly	Variable
Utilities	Electricity, water, etc.	$ 200.00	Monthly	Variable
Transportation	Gas, public transit	$ 150.00	Monthly	Variable
Entertainment	Streaming, outings	$ 50.00	Monthly	Variable
Variable Expenses Subtotal		**$ 750.00**		
Savings				
Emergency Fund	Short-term savings	$ 250.00	Monthly	Savings
Vacation Fund	Short-term savings	$ 100.00	Monthly	Savings
Retirement Fund	Long-term savings	$ 150.00	Monthly	Savings
Savings Subtotal		**$ 500.00**		
Total Balance		**$ 0.00**		

Managing excess funds or shortages within this approach requires you to strike a balance between flexibility and adherence to limits, in order to determine which categories can be the 'intermediary' without undermining primary financial responsibilities. Responsible redistribution is key. For example, if remaining grocery funds can cover unexpected car repairs, reallocate these instead of borrowing from categories earmarked for essential payments. By consciously balancing flexibility and adherence to limits, you keep your budget both dynamic and disciplined.

Adopting flexibility in budgeting involves recognizing how lifestyle changes impact finances. Major shifts, such as changing jobs, moving to a new city, or facing annual expenses like tuition fees or insurance premiums, necessitate recalibrating budgets. Job changes might mean adjusting income expectations; relocations can alter rent and utility costs significantly. Preparing yourself for potential curveballs ahead of time allows for smoother transitions, as you can adjust allocations in advance rather than reacting to financial strains later.

Regularly reviewing and adjusting your budget is essential, as expenses and income can change. Many people find budgeting apps like Mint or YNAB helpful for real-time tracking of spending, categorizing expenses, and seeing monthly trends. Envelope budgeting can also be adapted to digital formats using apps like Goodbudget that virtually replicate the envelope system's structure. These tools can make it easier to stay on budget and maintain financial discipline.

Regular budget reviews are fundamental to accommodating changes and fostering accountability. Aim to schedule these check-ins biweekly, monthly, or quarterly to compare your spending against your financial plan, identifying areas that may need adjustments or extra savings. Regular reviews keep your budget dynamic and aligned with your long-term goals, allowing you to make updates as needed. This practice encourages adaptability, strengthens budgeting discipline, and provides valuable opportunities to reflect on your spending habits. Through these reviews, you can celebrate progress toward your financial goals while addressing any challenges that may arise.

Choosing and Implementing Effective Budgeting Tools

Introducing saving into your world a dollar at a time seems intimidating, doesn't it? What steps can you take to have an easier transition from soliciting your parents' help to branching off into independence? Well, a convenient and effective instrument is probably sitting in your hand right now: your smartphone. Through the apps that you can download on your phone, you can practice effective budgeting even when you're on the go. In today's tech-savvy environment, a well-structured budget paired with digital budgeting tools is indispensable. These tools not only make managing finances easier but also cater to various financial habits and goals. Let's dive in and explore how these digital aids can transform your budgeting experience. With budgeting apps, there's a lot to choose from, each catering to different needs. Some popular options include YNAB, Goodbudget, EveryDollar, Empower Personal Wealth, PocketGuard, and Honeydue. YNAB, for instance, follows a zero-based budgeting system in which every dollar has a purpose even before it is earned—a hands-on approach that allows users to distribute their funds across categories like expenses, savings, and debt management (McMullen & Ayoola, 2024). Goodbudget uses an envelope system to help you allocate monthly income to specific spending areas. Although it requires manual input rather than connecting directly to your bank accounts, it provides a tangible way to plan and track finances meticulously.

For those who prefer a more integrated approach, Empower links to many accounts ranging from checking to credit cards, providing a comprehensive overview of your financial status. However, its strength lies in wealth tracking rather than detailed budgeting, making it ideal for individuals focused on investments and net worth monitoring. Next up, PocketGuard simplifies budgeting by showing what's left to spend after accounting for necessities, bills, and savings goals. PocketGuard is quite user-friendly, featuring automated tracking through account connections and manual input options for those who prefer more control over their data. Last but not least is Honeydue, an app worth considering if you're managing finances with a partner. You can share access to financial data while maintaining customizable privacy levels, making it ideal for joint budgeting without sacrificing individual autonomy.

While apps provide a convenient digital format for budgeting, spreadsheets offer unmatched flexibility and control. By using spreadsheet templates, you can tailor your budgeting process to suit your unique spending habits. It's fairly easy to customize your templates or use ones that already include formulas that automatically calculate totals, trends, and projections. These not only help you maintain current budgets but also guide you in understanding the underlying math behind financial planning. Ultimately, these tools foster a greater sense of awareness and accountability while enhancing your understanding of complex budgeting principles, such as cash flow analysis and forecasting.

In addition, websites like Mint and Personal Capital offer features beyond mere budgeting. You can set specific goals, track progress, set up automated reminders and notifications, and receive personalized insights through multiple reports. Also, you can take advantage of their educational content and community forums where you can share advice and experiences, as well as read about what worked for others.

The trick is to not get overwhelmed; as a matter of fact, choosing the right tool is easier than you think. If you prefer more control and granularity in tracking your finances, you can opt for manual spreadsheets; meanwhile, if you'd rather go for convenience and ease, you have a number of apps at your disposal. Experimenting with different approaches will help you find a system that feels easy to maintain.

In today's fast-paced world, financial management is often an overlooked aspect of relationships, yet it plays a lead role in a couple's overall well-being. The story of Mireille and Cassius serves as an enlightening example of how addressing financial differences can foster healthier dynamics and contribute to long-term partnership success. Like many couples, they initially struggled to align their financial philosophies, leading to misunderstanding and grievances that threatened to destabilize their relationship.

Mireille was an impulsive spender, often buying trendy clothes and dining out on a whim. In contrast, Cassius was more conservative with his expenditures, preferring to save for long-term investments and future stability. These differing mindsets created tension, as Mireille saw Cassius's frugality as overly restrictive, while Cassius perceived Mireille's spending habits as reckless. This divergence didn't merely affect their wallets; it also affected their emotional connection, introducing stress and frustration to their bond. Realizing that their financial disagreements were adversely affecting their relationship, they took action. They researched various budgeting applications and settled on one that allowed for both joint and individual budgeting. This decision marked a turning point in their financial dialogue. The app provided a clear, structured format for discussing their finances without the emotional weight of previous arguments. They could now see real-time data on their spending, set clear financial goals, and visualize their progress together.

The process of setting goals was transformative for Mireille and Cassius. They began by identifying shared priorities, such as planning for a vacation, purchasing a new car, and saving for a future home. By clearly outlining their combined goals, they created a sense of teamwork and collaboration that was previously lacking. Each goal was not just about numbers; it became a shared dream they both could work toward, fostering unity and cooperation.

The budgeting app that they chose allowed each of them to manage personal budgets for their individual expenses. This feature was highly instrumental in alleviating some of the friction in their relationship. Mireille appreciated having her own funds available for personal splurges without feeling guilty, while Cassius felt secure knowing that his savings goals weren't being compromised.

This dual budgeting system led to a significant decrease in disputes and arguments over spending, allowing them to appreciate the benefits of compromise and understanding. The improvement in their financial communication produced several positive outcomes. Mireille and Cassius discussed their monthly finances as a routine check-in, which diminished anxiety surrounding money.

These discussions became less about blame and more about strategic planning, setting the stage for more constructive dialogues. They explored each other's spending habits with a newfound respect, recognizing that both perspectives contributed to their partnership's overall strength. The joint budgeting app not only helped reduce financial stress but also allowed them to allocate more funds toward their shared goals.

Within 18 months, they successfully saved enough to take a well-deserved vacation to Costa Rica. This trip was not just a vacation; it symbolized their growth and the harmony they achieved through mutual understanding and collaboration.

The benefits of their financial journey extended beyond mere dollars and cents. Mireille and Cassius developed essential skills in negotiation and compromise, which bolstered their relationship in other areas as well. They learned to appreciate each other's values and priorities, leading to deeper conversations about their futures together. This stage marked a significant maturation of their relationship, as they navigated not just finances but also life goals and ambitions collectively.

Mireille and Cassius's journey underscores the vital role of financial management in romantic relationships. Over the course of 18 months, their communication regarding finances markedly improved, resulting in diminished tension and a more harmonious approach to their financial lives. Just as Mireille and Cassius have demonstrated, couples can effectively align their financial strategies.

This not only eases stress but also cultivates a stronger bond built on trust and cooperation. Their experience serves as an inspiring reminder that financial challenges can be resolved, leading to greater unity, shared victories, and a more balanced approach to managing both finances and relationships.

The Sum of Our Parts: Key Takeaways

In this chapter we learned to view budgeting as a vital tool for financial stability, emphasizing the importance of assigning each dollar a purpose before spending it. Budgeting is more than just a financial task; it's a roadmap to achieving goals, preventing unnecessary spending, and aligning expenses with personal priorities. We covered fundamental budgeting methods, like the 50/30/20 rule, which divides income into needs, wants, and savings, as well as practical strategies like the traditional envelope system. Both approaches provide structure and flexibility, helping users manage spending effectively.

Digital tools like YNAB, PocketGuard, and Goodbudget were revealed as valuable resources that make budgeting accessible and adaptable for different lifestyles. Each tool has unique features, from real-time expense tracking to automated categorization, which can simplify the budgeting process and support long-term financial goals.

Finally, flexibility is highlighted a cornerstone in budgeting, especially in adjusting for life changes like job transitions or relocations. Regular budget reviews are strongly suggested for maintaining alignment with financial goals. Through budgeting discipline and adaptability, you can reduce financial stress, take control of your finances, and build a path toward financial independence and peace. Budgeting, supported by the right tools, is your pathway to personal empowerment.

Chapter 4:

Saving Strategies and Preparing for the Unexpected

Strategic saving strategies are the backbone of financial preparedness, acting as both a cushion for unexpected events and a foundation for future security. It is possible to set yourself up for both short-term peace of mind and long-term prosperity. Having a robust saving plan is essential to give you the grace and time you need when unplanned medical expenses or a sudden loss of income occurs. Coming up, we'll explore the significance of approaching savings with a strategic mindset, building your savings effectively by establishing specific savings targets, understanding and prioritizing what matters most at different stages of your life, and crafting clear goals

Also, we'll look at logic-based emergency fund planning, which allows you to cultivate practical approaches to assembling a financial safety net. Then, we'll examine the benefits of utilizing high-yield savings accounts, highlighting how they can amplify your efforts through higher interest returns while maintaining easy access to your funds.

Setting Specific Savings Targets

Short-term goals encompass milestones you intend to achieve within a few years; these include saving for travel, tuition, or a more sophisticated phone or laptop. These goals require immediate attention and often come with more specific deadlines. Long-term goals, such as retirement planning, span over several decades. They involve strategic foresight and flexible timelines, and they can significantly impact financial planning. In addition, they entail different approaches and levels of commitment, allowing for adjustments as life changes occur. As a young adult, keeping this understanding in mind allows you to be better prepared and more diligent when allocating resources, depending on urgency and importance.

Incorporating smart goals lets you reap dividends. Consider the SMART Goals Framework for your financial planning, as it's highly effective. SMART stands for Specific, Measurable, Achievable, Relevant, and Time-bound—criteria that guide individuals in crafting precise and attainable financial objectives. For instance, instead of a vague goal like "save money," a SMART goal would be "save $15,000 for an international trip in two years." Setting a framework that focuses on measurable targets fosters a sense of pride, while a relevant goal aligns with broader financial aspirations and personal circumstances. How you prioritize your goals is important. Your first step should be to rank your savings objectives based on urgency, size, and personal significance. For example, paying off high-interest credit card debt might take precedence over saving for a vacation. Prioritization helps in focusing your efforts on what truly matters at any point, ensuring that critical financial needs are met without spreading your funds too thin. Using a simple ranking system or a list can help in this process, highlighting which goals require immediate attention and which can wait.

Setting regular benchmarks is another important strategy to sustain motivation and ensure commitment to saving habits. Regular reviews allow individuals to assess their progress, make necessary adjustments, celebrate minor victories, and remain engaged in their financial journey. For example, if you're saving for a down payment on a house, breaking it down into quarterly savings milestones can help track your advancement and adjust your plan if needed. Celebrating when reaching these benchmarks not only motivates you but also reinforces disciplined saving behaviors.

Financial goals are not static; they evolve with changing life circumstances. Life events such as getting a new job, moving to a new city, or starting a family require revisiting and potentially revising one's financial goals. Thus, it's essential to conduct regular assessments to keep goals aligned with current realities and future aspirations. This ongoing evaluation process becomes a part of life's rhythm, integrating financial planning seamlessly with personal growth and change. By defining clear goals and integrating strategies like the SMART framework, prioritization, and regular benchmarking, individuals can navigate their financial paths with greater certainty and confidence. These practices help build a foundation for lifelong financial literacy, equipping individuals with the tools needed to adapt to economic shifts and personal developments. Here's an example of the commitment and strategic thinking that go into saving financial resources. Lauren-Grace had recently graduated and set a clear aspiration to accumulate $10,000 for the purchase of a car within two years. To attain this goal, she applied the SMART criteria, ensuring her strategy was precise and practical. Lauren-Grace articulated her goal with precision: She aimed to save $10,000 specifically for acquiring a vehicle. This aim was well-defined, addressing her urgent requirement for dependable transportation necessary for commuting to work and managing essential daily tasks.

To effectively monitor her savings journey, Lauren-Grace established a concrete benchmark. She calculated that, to reach her target within the designated two years, she would need to save approximately $416.67 monthly. This specific figure enabled her to track her progress clearly and maintain her motivation consistently. A thorough understanding of her financial landscape was vital for Lauren-Grace. She began by outlining a detailed budget encompassing her entire monthly income and expenditures. After analyzing her spending habits, she pinpointed nonessential expenses, such as dining out and subscription services, which she could cut back on or temporarily eliminate. By refining her financial habits, she ensured that her savings aspiration remained realistic and achievable. Lauren-Grace's initiative to save for a car was closely aligned with her need for dependable transportation.

With a new job that required daily commuting, she understood that owning a vehicle would not only enhance her autonomy but also open the door to broader employment opportunities in the long run. This significance fueled her resolve toward achieving her goal. By establishing a two-year deadline for her savings target, Lauren-Grace cultivated a sense of urgency that motivated her progress. Each month, she took responsibility for her savings, ensuring she remained on track towards achieving her goal. With this structured approach, she meticulously recorded her progress, celebrated every milestone achieved, and ultimately reached her financial ambition with newfound confidence. This strategy not only enabled her to save the desired amount but also fostered a sense of discipline and accomplishment that she carried into future pursuits.

This story illustrates how clear goals, careful financial planning, and a commitment to disciplined habits can catalyze personal growth and success. It's a powerful reminder of how organized planning and focused effort can lead to significant life changes.

Lauren-Grace's journey not only embodies financial responsibility but also serves as a case study for all who seek to achieve substantial goals with determination and strategy.

The Power of Setting SMART Financial Goals: Crafting Specific, Measurable, Achievable, Relevant, and Time-Bound Plans

Setting financial goals is essential to gaining control over your financial future, but creating effective goals requires more than just ambition. SMART goals, which stand for Specific, Measurable, Achievable, Relevant, and Time-Bound, provide a structured framework that breaks down large financial ambitions into manageable and actionable steps.

Whether you're saving for an emergency fund, planning for a vacation, or building a retirement nest egg, SMART goals can help you focus your efforts and track progress systematically.

Understanding SMART Goals: A Step-by-Step Guide

The SMART approach to goal-setting makes your financial plans clear and actionable. Each component of SMART contributes to building a goal that is both practical and motivating.

1. Specific: Define the exact amount or target you want to achieve. A specific goal gives you a clear direction, making it easier to formulate a plan.

2. Measurable: Assigning a quantifiable measure to your goal lets you track your progress and see how close you are to completion.

3. Achievable: Setting a realistic target ensures that your goal is within reach, given your current financial situation.

4. Relevant: Aligning your goal with your broader life priorities keeps you motivated and prevents you from

pursuing objectives that don't serve your long-term interests.

5. Time-Bound: Set a deadline to create a sense of urgency, which can keep you focused and committed.

Crafting Your SMART Goals

Let's break down each part of a SMART goal with examples to illustrate how to apply this framework effectively.

1. Specific

Instead of a vague goal like "save money," create a specific target. For example, "Save $6,000 for a down payment on a car."

Example: Janelle wants to purchase a used car within the next year. Rather than simply aiming to save more, she specifies that her goal is to save $6,000 as a down payment. This specific figure helps her stay focused and gives her a concrete purpose for her savings.

2. Measurable

A measurable goal includes benchmarks that allow you to track progress. Breaking down the $6,000 into monthly contributions provides a clear savings path.

Example: Janelle decides to save $500.00 each month, a measurable and trackable amount that helps her evaluate her progress and adjust her spending if needed. She tracks her savings in a budgeting app, providing a visual reminder of her progress.

3. Achievable

Goals should stretch your abilities without being unrealistic. To determine whether saving $6,000 in a year is achievable, Janelle assesses her income, monthly expenses, and existing obligations.

Example: Janelle has a stable income and identifies discretionary expenses she can reduce, such as dining out and entertainment, to make her monthly savings target achievable. This helps her stay motivated and realistic about her goal.

4. Relevant

A goal must be personally meaningful and aligned with broader financial objectives.

Example: Janelle's goal of buying a car is directly tied to her career, as it will enable her to commute more efficiently. Knowing this adds relevance to her goal, increasing her commitment to achieving it.

5. Time-Bound

Setting a timeline creates urgency and establishes a plan with a definite end point.

Example: Janelle's target is to save $6,000 within a year. By setting this deadline, she can assess her progress each month, keeping herself accountable.

Applying SMART Goals to Financial Milestones

SMART goals are versatile and can be applied to various financial ambitions, from short-term purchases to long-term investments.

Here are additional examples to illustrate how SMART goals can work for other financial priorities:

1. Emergency Fund

- Goal: "Save $1,500 in six months for an emergency fund."

- Plan: Set aside $250 each month by reallocating non-essential spending.

- Outcome: With a fully funded emergency account, you gain a financial buffer against unexpected expenses, reducing financial stress.

2. Vacation Savings

- Goal: "Save $3,000 for a summer vacation over the next 12 months."

- Plan: Put away $250 per month by cutting back on luxury expenses like eating out.

- Outcome: Enjoy a guilt-free vacation knowing it was fully funded in advance, without impacting regular finances.

3. Debt Repayment

- Goal: "Pay off $2,000 of credit card debt in 10 months."

- Plan: Contribute $200 per month by budgeting carefully and reducing discretionary purchases.

- Outcome: Reduced debt burden and improved credit score through a structured approach to repayment.

Tools to Help Track and Manage SMART Goals

Today's technology makes it easier than ever to set, track, and achieve SMART financial goals. Numerous apps and tools are designed to support financial goal-setting with specific features.

- Budgeting Apps: Apps like Mint and YNAB offer visual dashboards to track your goals and categorize expenses, helping you stay within budget and redirect savings towards your objectives.

- Savings Calculators: Online calculators allow you to visualize how long it will take to reach a goal based on your monthly savings rate and can be helpful in setting realistic time frames.

- Investment Tools: For long-term goals, investment apps like Acorns or Betterment offer automated investing, allowing users to contribute regularly to investment accounts designed to grow their funds over time.

Example: Aaron uses Mint to track his progress towards a $10,000 emergency fund. With each paycheck, he contributes $300, watching the balance grow in his savings account tracker. By viewing his progress in real-time, he remains motivated and on track.

Overcoming Obstacles with SMART Goals

Even with well-defined goals, financial challenges and unexpected expenses may arise. An important aspect of maintaining progress is adjusting your SMART goals as circumstances change.

1. Revise Time Frames: If you encounter a setback, consider extending your timeline slightly to relieve financial pressure while still working towards your goal.

2. Break Down Further: If a monthly target is challenging, switch to smaller, weekly contributions to make it more manageable.

3. Celebrate Milestones: Acknowledge small victories, such as reaching half of your goal, to maintain motivation.

Example: When Sarah had to replace her laptop unexpectedly, she had to dip into her car savings. She adjusted her timeline by two months and broke down her contributions into weekly amounts to get back on track.

Why SMART Goals Foster Financial Independence

Setting SMART goals promotes self-discipline and financial responsibility, essential qualities for achieving financial independence. By establishing clear objectives and tracking them, you cultivate habits that help prevent impulsive spending and ensure your money is directed towards meaningful purposes.

SMART goals also serve as a tool for measuring growth over time. As you achieve smaller objectives, you build confidence to tackle larger financial goals, creating a sustainable pathway to financial security and freedom.

Incorporating SMART financial goals into your life isn't just about achieving immediate savings targets or debt reduction; it's about creating a mindset that values long-term stability. By mastering this structured approach to financial planning, you position yourself for success in any financial endeavor, equipping yourself with the skills to adapt to future financial challenges with confidence.

Various Savings Strategies

If you are just beginning your savings journey, adopting a structured savings strategy can create a solid foundation for long-term financial stability. Here are three effective approaches, each offering a unique perspective on managing money and setting aside funds for the future.

1. The 50/30/20 Rule

The 50/30/20 rule is a popular method for dividing income into three major categories: necessities, discretionary spending, and savings or debt repayment. As mentioned earlier, this approach involves allocating 50% of income to essential expenses (housing, groceries), 30% to wants (dining, entertainment), and 20% to savings or debt reduction (Warren & Tyagi, 2005). For example, if Jamie earns $3,000 per month, he would dedicate $1,500 to rent and food, $900 to personal enjoyment, and $600 toward building his savings. This structured approach provides financial stability while allowing some freedom for non-essential purchases.

The 50/30/20 rule's simplicity makes it a great starting point for young adults, as it balances basic living expenses with room for fun, while still prioritizing future financial goals.

2. Pay Yourself First

David Bach's The Automatic Millionaire introduces the concept of "paying yourself first," a strategy focused on building savings automatically. This method involves setting aside a specific percentage of income—often 10-15%—for savings before paying other expenses (Bach, 2016). Automating this savings transfer each month ensures that you consistently contribute to your financial goals without being tempted to spend first and save later.

For instance, Kristina, who earns $2,500 per month, sets up an automatic transfer of 10% ($250) to a high-yield savings account. This way, even if she has unexpected expenses, she is already saving for her future. Over time, this disciplined approach helps build a healthy financial cushion and encourages the habit of prioritizing savings.

This strategy is particularly helpful for individuals who struggle with consistency, as automated contributions eliminate the temptation to skip savings for the month.

3. Goal-Based Savings Buckets

Ramit Sethi's I Will Teach You to Be Rich introduces the idea of creating separate savings "buckets" for specific financial goals. Rather than saving in one general account, Sethi suggests dividing funds into different categories, such as an emergency fund, short-term purchases (like a vacation or gadget), and long-term investments (Sethi, 2009).

Each "bucket" can be tracked individually, which maintains motivation by showing progress toward each goal. Consider Eric, who earns $3,500 per month. He allocates $200 to his emergency fund, $100 toward a new laptop, and $150 to his retirement account. By seeing how each bucket grows monthly, Eric stays motivated and financially organized. This method also helps him avoid dipping into long-term savings for impulsive purchases, as he has separate funds for different goals.

Goal-based savings buckets are especially effective for those juggling multiple goals, allowing them to save with purpose and clarity. Digital banking tools make this strategy even easier by allowing users to create multiple savings "buckets" within one account.

These three savings strategies—the 50/30/20 rule, paying yourself first, and goal-based buckets—offer versatile solutions for you to consider as you start your financial journey. Each method fosters discipline, builds consistency, and supports various financial goals, creating a foundation for long-term wealth growth. Through regular savings, automated contributions, and goal-oriented planning, you can build financial resilience and prepare for future milestones.

Supercharging Your Savings: Building Your Emergency Fund With High-Yield Savings Accounts

Begin by calculating essential monthly expenses such as housing, utilities, groceries, and healthcare costs. Multiply this sum by the number of months you wish to cover, ensuring that your fund is as comprehensive as possible. How much to save for your protective buffer requires careful consideration of your lifestyle and financial responsibilities. Many financial experts recommend having at least three months' worth of living expenses set aside. If you are self-employed, work seasonally, or have dependents, aim for a minimum of eight months to a year to cover additional risks.

Consistency is key. Automate your savings. The more manageable the chunks, the easier it would be to manage your savings. Setting up automatic transfers from your checking to savings makes it easy to set your goal and forget it. Here's what you shouldn't forget: Start small, and set aside what you can afford to save, usually around $2,000. Laying a sound foundation will motivate you to continue saving.

High-yield savings accounts (HYSAs) present a strategic option for maximizing the growth of your emergency fund. Unlike traditional savings accounts, HYSAs typically offer higher interest rates and more flexibility, making them an attractive choice for savers seeking to optimize their returns. The increased interest means that your money grows more efficiently over time, allowing you to reach your savings goals faster. Also, HYSAs provide you with easy access to your funds; they ensure that, if you need your money, it's only a withdrawal away.

As you're researching, check out online banks and credit unions. They usually offer higher interest rates, thanks to their reduced operational costs compared to traditional brick-and-mortar banks. Look for competitive interest rates and evaluate account features, such as fees, minimum balance requirements, and withdrawal limits. Avoid accounts that charge unnecessary fees or impose penalties for accessing your savings. By investing your emergency fund into a HYSA, you gain improved returns while enjoying the convenience of tracking and managing your money. It can also help reduce any urges you may have to access your account for non-emergency needs. Building an emergency fund goes a long way to support long-term financial stability. Celebrate milestones, such as tax refunds or bonuses, to give your savings a boost.

The Sum of Our Parts: Key Takeaways

In this chapter, we emphasize the importance of strategic savings in creating both short-term security and long-term financial stability. By prioritizing savings with a structured approach, you not only safeguard against unforeseen expenses, like medical bills or income loss, but also lay a foundation for future goals.

I encourage you to adopt a strategic mindset in setting clear savings targets. These targets are divided into short-term goals, like vacations or electronics, and long-term goals, such as retirement, each requiring tailored commitment and flexibility as circumstances evolve. The SMART Goals Framework— Specific, Measurable, Achievable, Relevant, and Time-Bound— is highlighted as a powerful tool in setting actionable financial objectives. This framework helps build clarity and motivation, transforming abstract goals into concrete achievements. For example, instead of vaguely aiming to "save money," a SMART goal might be "save $15,000 for an international trip in two years," making the objective clear and measurable.

Prioritizing savings goals based on urgency, such as paying off high-interest debts before planning vacations, helps maximize the effectiveness of your savings. Regular benchmarks allow for tracking progress, celebrating small wins, and making adjustments. This dynamic approach not only boosts motivation but also helps embed disciplined saving behaviors.

We've also explored various savings strategies to meet these goals, such as the 50/30/20 rule (dividing income into necessities, discretionary spending, and savings), "pay yourself first" (automatically saving a percentage of income before spending), and goal-based savings buckets (allocating funds to distinct purposes). High-yield savings accounts are recommended for building emergency funds, offering higher interest rates while maintaining accessibility, especially with online banks and credit unions.

Ultimately, regular assessments and adjusting savings plans to align with life changes ensure that financial goals stay relevant and achievable. Through clear goals, strategic planning, and disciplined habits, individuals are equipped to handle financial challenges confidently and secure their financial futures.

Money Smarts: A Practical Guide to Financial Independence for Young Adults

"The best way to find yourself is to lose yourself in the service of others." - Mahatma Gandhi

Helping others can make life brighter for everyone. That's why I'm reaching out to you to make a difference!

Would you take a moment to help someone just like you—someone curious about handling money better but not quite sure where to begin?

My goal with *Money Smarts* is to make learning about money easy, interesting, and practical. But to reach more people, I need your help.

Most of us pick books based on reviews, and that's where you come in. By leaving a review, you can help another young adult just like you who wants to make smarter money choices but needs a little guidance to get started.

Your review could help...
>...one more young adult learn the basics of budgeting.
>...one more person find a way to save for their dreams.
>...one more student feel confident about their financial future.
>...one more reader discover practical steps to independence.

It takes just a moment but can make a big difference in someone's financial journey. To leave a review, simply scan the QR code below, or visit **https://www.amazon.com/review/review-your-purchases/?asin=B0DNG94FKX**

If you love helping others, you're my kind of person. Thank you from the bottom of my heart!

Renae C Linde

Chapter 5:

Investment Fundamentals for Young Adults

Understanding investment fundamentals is an essential skill for young adults laying a solid foundation for financial independence. It's a powerful tool for building wealth and achieving long-term goals. It involves making informed decisions about where to allocate resources to grow one's finances. Beyond the prospect of monetary gain, investing requires a combination of knowledge, patience, and strategy. It's time now to examine the various investment options available to you, each presenting unique opportunities and risks. We will explore traditional avenues like stocks and bonds, understanding how they function and the returns you can expect. We'll examine modern investments such as mutual funds and exchange-traded funds (ETFs), particularly their benefits in terms of diversification and risk management.

In the end, you will be equipped with helpful insights into evaluating potential investments and managing associated risks, thus encouraging active participation in community-based financial ventures and fostering confidence in starting your investment journey.

Investments, What's the Big Deal?

Investing early in long-term growth funds leverages the power of compound interest, a concept Albert Einstein famously described as the "eighth wonder of the world." By consistently reinvesting earnings, investors allow their money to grow at an accelerating pace, as each cycle of returns is calculated on a continually increasing base. Starting young gives an investor more "cycles" of compounding, leading to exponential growth over time.

For example, consider two friends, Sherry and Brittney. Sherry starts investing $200 per month in a growth fund at age 25, earning an average annual return of 7%. By age 65, Sherry's total contributions of $96,000 will have grown to over $500,000 due to compounded returns. Brittney, however, starts the same investment plan at 35. Despite contributing the same $200 per month until age 65, Brittney's investment only grows to about

$245,000. Those ten extra years allowed Sherry to nearly double Brittney's final balance.

Choosing Growth Funds Wisely

Long-term growth funds, like index funds or exchange-traded funds (ETFs) that track broad markets, are particularly well-suited for compound growth. Vanguard's S&P 500 ETF (VOO), for example, has averaged approximately 10% annual returns since its inception, though it fluctuates with the market (Morningstar, 2023).

Diversified funds minimize risk by spreading investments across numerous companies, reducing the impact of any one company's performance on the overall fund. Growth-oriented funds tend to include more stocks than bonds, capitalizing on stocks' potential for higher returns over the long term.

Taking Advantage of Tax-Advantaged Accounts

Another way to amplify long-term investments is by using tax-advantaged accounts, like a Roth IRA. In a Roth IRA, investments grow tax-free, meaning all gains from compounding are untaxed upon withdrawal in retirement (IRS, 2023).

For example, if Emma's $500,000 balance were in a Roth IRA, she could withdraw her funds tax-free at age 65, maximizing her wealth compared to a taxable account.

Starting early, choosing the right funds, and leveraging tax-advantaged accounts all play an important role in harnessing the full potential of compounding. By using these strategies, you can create a pathway to long-term financial security and potentially retire comfortably, knowing you've given your money the maximum time and structure to grow.

The Power of Compounding Over Time

Compounding is one of the most powerful concepts in investing, and its impact grows exponentially over time. Here's how it works and why it becomes especially powerful over decades. Compounding occurs when your investments earn returns, and those returns are reinvested, earning additional returns themselves. For example, if you invest $1,000 at an annual return rate of 7.5%, in one year, you'll have $1,075. The next year, you earn 7.5% not just on the original $1,000 but on the $1,075, leading to a faster growth rate.

When you start investing early, your money has more time to compound, leading to exponential growth. The longer you stay invested, the more powerful compounding becomes. For example, after 10 years your initial investment might double or slightly more than double. After 30 years, the same investment grows much more than it did during the first decade. The amount of growth during the last decade alone is typically far greater than what you initially invested.

Time is your best ally. Consider this example with $200 a month at 7.5%. If you invest $200/month starting at age 20, by age 65, your investment will have grown tremendously compared to starting at age 40. Starting early gives your investments decades of compounding returns, and the effect accelerates with each passing year. By contrast, starting late limits how much time your money has to grow.

The compounding effect is not linear; it follows an exponential curve. This means that in the later years of your investment journey, the value can grow significantly faster than in the early years. Delaying investing by even a decade can result in a significantly smaller end balance because you miss out on the compounding effect over those years. This is why starting to invest as early as possible, even if it's a small amount, is so critical. Compounding also helps combat inflation. As prices rise over time, compounded investment growth can outpace the erosion of purchasing power due to inflation.

Early and consistent investing allows for maximum compounding over time. Each dollar invested early has the potential to grow many times over due to this effect, leading to substantial wealth accumulation over decades.

Here is a chart that illustrates compounding over time where Sharon starts investing 10 years earlier than Jerry.

Year (starting from decade 1)	Sharon	Jerry
1	$ 2,500	$ -
2	$ 5,194	$ -
3	$ 8,097	$ -
4	$ 11,225	$ -
5	$ 14,596	$ -
6	$ 18,229	$ -
7	$ 22,144	$ -
8	$ 26,363	$ -
9	$ 30,909	$ -
10	$ 35,808	$ -
11	$ 41,088	$ 2,500
12	$ 46,778	$ 5,194
13	$ 52,909	$ 8,097
14	$ 59,516	$ 11,225
15	$ 66,636	$ 14,596
16	$ 74,309	$ 18,229
17	$ 82,578	$ 22,144
18	$ 91,488	$ 26,363
19	$ 101,091	$ 30,909
20	$ 111,438	$ 35,808

Year (starting from decade 1)	Sharon	Jerry
21	$ 122,589	$ 41,088
22	$ 134,606	$ 46,778
23	$ 147,556	$ 52,909
24	$ 161,511	$ 59,516
25	$ 176,549	$ 66,636
26	$ 192,754	$ 74,309
27	$ 210,218	$ 82,578
28	$ 229,038	$ 91,488
29	$ 249,318	$ 101,091
30	$ 271,173	$ 111,438

Evaluating Investment Options and Risk Management

When you think about investing, it's important to evaluate various choices to find what suits your needs and risk tolerance. Let's start by discussing stocks. These represent ownership in a company and provide the opportunity for long-term growth. When you purchase a share of stock, you're essentially buying a small piece of that business. If the company performs well, the value of your shares may increase, potentially resulting in profits when sold. Some stocks pay dividends, which are portions of the company's earnings distributed to shareholders.

Investing in stocks requires careful research into the company's performance, industry trends, and broader economic factors. It's important to note that stocks are often subject to market volatility—meaning their prices can fluctuate significantly over short periods. Volatility can cause quick gains but also substantial losses, making them more suitable for those who can tolerate such fluctuations.

Moving on, bonds are appealing to investors seeking stable and predictable returns. Bonds are less volatile compared to stocks and are considered safer investments. A bond represents a loan made by an investor to a borrower, typically a corporation or government. In return for this loan, the borrower promises to pay back the principal amount on a future date and provides regular interest payments.

Risk-averse investors find bonds suitable because they offer lower volatility. However, they're not without risk. Factors like interest rate changes, inflation, and the financial health of the issuer can influence bond values. For example, if interest rates rise, existing bonds with lower rates may decrease in value.

If you are open to the idea of diversifying your investments but lack the capital or time to manage an extensive portfolio, mutual funds and ETFs might appeal to you. Mutual funds pool money from many investors to purchase a diversified collection of stocks, bonds, or other securities. Managed by professional fund managers, mutual funds aim to achieve specific financial objectives based on the fund's strategy. One of their primary advantages is diversification, reducing the risk associated with individual stock selection.

When selecting investment options, consider your financial goals, time horizon, and risk tolerance. While stocks may suit younger individuals looking for growth opportunities, bonds provide stability for those seeking minimal risk. ETFs offer a unique investment avenue, functioning similarly to mutual funds but allowing for trading on stock exchanges. This capability enables investors to buy and sell throughout the trading day, fostering a dynamic approach to managing their portfolios.

Many ETFs mirror the performance of prominent indices, such as the S&P 500, thus granting investors access to wide segments of the market while keeping costs relatively low. With their inherent diversification, both mutual funds and ETFs serve as excellent starting points for novice investors seeking to grow their wealth.

One interesting example would be Liam and his roommate Noah, both recent college graduates navigating their financial futures. After graduation, Liam embraced a traditional investment strategy, allocating his savings primarily to mutual funds. He appreciated the steady management and perceived stability these funds offered, believing they would provide a reliable foundation for his financial security. Noah, however, took a different route. Intrigued by the flexibility and transparency of ETFs, he invested a portion of his funds in several high-performing, sector-focused ETFs.

He quickly learned how to analyze market trends and individual fund performances, eagerly trading throughout the day to optimize his investments. As they both tracked their progress, they found themselves in a friendly rivalry, often sharing insights and strategies over dinner. Liam would highlight the long-term potential of his mutual funds, emphasizing their historical performance and consistency. Meanwhile, Noah would show how his ETF portfolio allowed him to react swiftly to market changes, capitalizing on daily fluctuations while still maintaining exposure to broad market trends.

Gradually, both realized that their respective strategies had merit, but they also recognized the limitations inherent in each approach. Liam noticed that his mutual funds had higher expense ratios than he initially thought, eating into his returns. Conversely, Noah faced challenges in managing the risks associated with his more frequent trading, feeling the strains of emotional decision-making. This led Liam to explore the possibility of incorporating ETFs into his investment strategy, as he was intrigued by the potential for greater liquidity and lower fees.

Noah began considering the virtues of mutual funds, particularly with long-term stability and professional management. Together, they researched ways to create a balanced investment portfolio that blended the strengths of both vehicles. Through their experiences, Liam and Noah learned the value of adaptability in investing. They realized that neither mutual funds nor ETFs alone would encompass all their financial goals. By combining their knowledge and leveraging the unique advantages of each, they could construct a more resilient investment strategy.

Their journey underscored an important lesson for many new investors: The key to successful investing often lies in understanding the nuances of different investment vehicles and finding a balance that aligns with individual risk tolerance and financial objectives. As both roommates continued to refine their investment strategies, they grew not just as investors but as friends, dedicated to supporting each other's financial journeys while navigating the complexities of the investment world together.

Strategies for Mitigating Investment Risks

Investing can be an intimidating venture, particularly for you as a young adult starting out. To ease your concerns and prepare yourself for a prosperous financial journey, you need to understand strategies that can minimize the risks associated with investing. Let's explore some key concepts, including risk tolerance assessment, diversification, thorough research, and regular portfolio review.

It's wise to evaluate your individual risk appetite before making investment decisions. Risk appetite describes how much risk you will assume in your investments, and it's uniquely personal, differing from person to person. Choosing multiple online assessments can help you determine your risk appetite by examining factors like age, income, financial responsibilities, and investment objectives. These tools empower you to make informed choices that align your comfort level with your risk tolerance. Recognizing your risk appetite helps you avoid impulsive decisions driven by market fluctuations or social influence, preventing potential stress or financial setbacks.

Another essential strategy for reducing investment risks is diversification. Forget concentrating all your investments in a single area—diversification entails allocating your resources across various asset classes. This technique can cushion against losses, as underperformance in one segment can be offset by gains in another.

For instance, investing only in one company's stock carries the risk of total loss if that stock declines. A more prudent strategy involves spreading investments across multiple companies in different sectors, along with bonds, real estate, and mutual funds, thus distributing risk. While this method doesn't eliminate risk, it can lessen the effects of major market fluctuations. This approach doesn't eliminate risk entirely, but it can reduce the impact of significant market swings. According to Ameriprise Financial (2024), diversification across asset classes can relieve the blow of major market fluctuations.

Before investing, conduct research and familiarize yourself with current market trends and economic indicators like inflation rates, interest rates, and employment statistics, which can influence market behavior. Diving into company-specific data, such as earnings reports, leadership, competitive standing, and future prospects, provides insight into potential investment performance. Understanding these aspects helps you make informed decisions rather than relying on hearsay or assumptions. Thorough research equips you with clarity and confidence, reducing the probability of hasty decisions based on incomplete information.

Regular reviews allow you to realign your portfolio according to changing values, objectives, and/or market conditions. Suppose a particular sector experiences a downturn; reallocation might be necessary to maintain portfolio health. As you progress and accumulate wealth, you may switch gears and go for higher-risk investments for growth, thus necessitating critical readjustments in your portfolio. Allowing flexibility in your investments assures alignment with both your short-term needs and long-term goals.

How? You should start by using reliable, well-vetted advice, such as talking to financial advisors or asking them to recommend online resources designed to map risk profiles. Setting aside dedicated time for staying informed about market news and updates ensures continuity in your knowledge acquisition To diversify, limit your investments in any single asset or security; this prevents overexposure to one type of asset, thus balancing risk. Lastly, establishing a consistent schedule to review your portfolio, either every three or six months, enables you to be proactive and responsive to any changes.

The Sum of Our Parts: Key Takeaways

Now you've been provided with a comprehensive introduction to investment fundamentals, tailored to help you build wealth and achieve financial independence. By examining a range of traditional and modern investment options—such as stocks, bonds, mutual funds, and ETFs — you've gained insights into the risks and returns associated with each. Growth funds and the power of compound interest were highlighted, demonstrating how early investments grow exponentially over time, especially when using tax-advantaged accounts like Roth IRAs.

We've illustrated the significance of evaluating one's risk tolerance, diversifying investments, and conducting thorough research to manage risks effectively. Practical examples, like the stories of Sherry and Brittney or roommates Liam and Noah, underscore how different investment strategies align with individual financial goals and risk preferences. Additionally, strategies like regular portfolio reviews and goal-setting provide you with a structured approach to adapt your investments as life circumstances and market conditions change.

Through these fundamentals, I encourage you to approach investing with confidence, leveraging early investments, strategic diversification, and continuous learning to establish a resilient path toward financial growth and security. By understanding these concepts, you can make informed, empowered decisions, setting the stage for lifelong financial stability and independence.

Chapter 6:

Avoiding Financial Pitfalls -

Scams and Schemes

Recognizing and avoiding financial scams is a skill you need in our increasingly connected world. The digital age opens up vast opportunities but also exposes you to countless risks, particularly as a young adult who is often targeted by deceptive schemes. Scams can appear harmless on the surface, but they can lead to serious financial damage if not identified early. From seemingly innocuous emails to investment proposals that promise sky-high returns, these pitfalls lure you into losing your hard-earned money.

Understanding these scams puts power back in your hands, allowing you to navigate the complexities of financial independence with confidence. You'll learn how to spot phishing attempts that often lurk in your emails or social media messages, discern telltale signs of fraudulent investment offers, and implement strategies to secure your online transactions. By comparing legitimate practices with scam indicators, you'll be equipped with the knowledge to make informed decisions and safeguard your finances. Whether you're just managing your own money or helping others become financially literate, the insights offered here will serve as valuable tools in your financial tool kit.

Recognizing Online Phishing Tactics

Phishing attempts are common traps that cybercriminals use to exploit unsuspecting individuals. Understanding how these scams operate and what signs to look out for can save you from devastating losses. Let's dive into how you can detect phishing attempts and secure your data effectively.

In spotting phishing emails, one of the primary indicators is poor grammar and unusual sender addresses. Legitimate companies typically have a professional communication style and make sure their emails are grammatically correct. If you receive an email filled with typos or awkward sentence structures, consider it a red flag. Often, such errors result from poor translation or deliberate attempts to avoid spam filters (Microsoft, 2021). The sender's email address can tell a lot about the message's authenticity. Pay attention to mismatched domains or subtle changes in the domain name, like replacing letters with similar-looking numbers or characters. For instance, seeing "micros0ft.com" instead of "microsoft.com" is a sign of a forgery (Microsoft, 2021).

These tactics deceive recipients into believing emails are from trusted sources. Another important aspect to watch out for is unknown links or attachments within emails. They frequently hide malicious software that can steal your sensitive information. Before clicking on any link, hover over it to see the actual URL. Does it match the company's legitimate web address? On mobile devices, pressing and holding the link will reveal its true destination (Microsoft, 2021). Similarly, be cautious about unexpected attachments, especially if they come with extensions commonly associated with malware, like .exe, .zip, or .scr files (Cofense, n.d.). It's always better to verify the source before downloading anything onto your device.

Social media has become intricately woven into the fabric of our daily existence, serving as a double-edged sword that can expose us to a myriad of scams. You have to stay alert when receiving friend requests or messages from unfamiliar accounts. Scammers frequently create deceptive profiles to infiltrate your personal space, seeking access to sensitive information or redirecting you to phony websites. To guard yourself effectively, make it a habit to check who can view your shared content and maintain updated privacy settings. If a request or message triggers a sense of unease or appears abnormal, it's prudent to disregard or report it.

In a typical corporate environment, Ava, William, Riley, Elliot, and Cameron—all in their mid-20s—showcase the complexities of navigating social connections, including those formed in digital spheres. Ava, a marketing associate, uses TikTok to build her professional brand, sharing insights into effective digital strategies. However, she has encountered various aspects of social media that have raised her awareness about potential risks. One afternoon, while browsing her Instagram feed, Ava received a follow request from an account claiming to be a well-known industry influencer. Intrigued, she accepted the request, thinking it could help her network. Later, she received a direct message from this account, asking for sensitive information about her marketing campaigns and cloaking the request under the guise of collaboration. Ava's instincts kicked in, and she researched the account, soon realizing it was a fabricated profile with misleading information. This incident reinforced her understanding that even seemingly harmless connections could be misleading.

William, working in finance, has had his fair share of encounters with social media fraud. He uses LinkedIn extensively for professional networking, but he was recently subjected to a phishing attack. An account, masquerading as a reputable financial firm, sent him a message about an exclusive investment opportunity. Lured by the seemingly lucrative offer, he almost clicked the provided link, which would have led him to a fraudulent page designed to steal his credentials. Luckily, he hesitated and consulted colleagues, leading to an important discussion about the significance of verifying the legitimacy of online communications.

Riley, an IT specialist, often advises her coworkers on security protocols. She recently organized a workshop focused on recognizing potential scams and safeguarding personal information online. As part of her presentation, she shared real-life cases of clients duped by sophisticated schemes that exploited social media. Her practical advice emphasized the necessity of scrutinizing any requests for information and using two-factor authentication for accounts. By sharing these insights, she created a stronger sense of security awareness among her peers, encouraging them to cultivate a culture of skepticism regarding social media interactions.

Elliot, a graphic designer, thrives on creativity and connection. His vibrant Instagram showcases his work, but it also draws a fair share of attention from scammers. He constantly receives messages from purported clients asking for portfolio reviews or offers for collaborations. One day, he received a convincing message from someone claiming to be a director at a prestigious advertising agency. They requested samples of his work, along with personal details. Having heard Riley's workshop insights, Elliot investigated further. After a few suspicious exchanges, he found inconsistencies that revealed the account was fake.

Cameron, a sales representative, harnesses social media to promote his products. He keeps his profiles professional, but even he has fallen prey to a fake profile that copied his data and began reaching out to his contacts, requesting funds for a "charitable cause." It caused confusion among his friends and colleagues until Cameron addressed the issue openly. He educated his network about reporting fake profiles, underlining how quickly misinformation can spread and advising everyone to verify requests, particularly those sent from profiles that seem odd.

Through these experiences, this group of mid-20s coworkers exemplifies how awareness and education can empower individuals to navigate the treacherous waters of social media. Each incident highlights the necessity for ongoing discussions about cybersecurity and the proactive measures one can take to protect oneself from various online risks. By fostering a culture of awareness, Ava, William, Riley, Elliot, and Cameron are not just protecting themselves but also advocating for their peers. Building connections online can be beneficial, but it should always be balanced with caution, clear judgment, and a healthy dose of skepticism.

Security Check-Ins

To further improve your security, it's important to follow established methods. Implementing two-factor authentication

(2FA) adds an extra layer of protection to your accounts. This method requires a secondary form of verification, such as a code sent to your phone or an authentication app, making it harder for hackers to gain unauthorized access even if they have your password. Similarly, setting strong, unique passwords and changing them regularly can minimize the risk of a breach. Avoid using easily guessable passwords like birthdates or simple word combinations. Besides monitoring, using strong password practices enhances your financial security. Avoid using simple passwords or reusing them across multiple sites. Opt for combinations that include upper- and lower-case letters, numbers, and symbols to increase complexity. Change passwords periodically to minimize the risk of breaches. Using password managers can help you maintain and organize complex passwords without the hassle of memorizing them. Thus, investing a little time in creating complex passwords can go a long way in ensuring your safety.

Besides these methods, staying informed about recent phishing techniques can help you recognize any developing threats. Cybercriminals continually change their strategies to trick users, so keeping up-to-date with cybersecurity news is beneficial. Taking part in online workshops or sessions on digital security can also equip you with practical knowledge to fend off potential attacks.

If you suspect you've been targeted or you accidentally fell for a phishing scam, act swiftly. Change the passwords of all affected accounts immediately, and enable multifactor authentication if not already active. Keep a record of any details you remember from the attack, like sender information or suspicious links, as they might be useful if you need to report the incident. Notifying IT support at school or work, in case your work-related accounts are compromised, is also advisable. They can help you take further measures to safeguard your data. If there's a possibility of identity theft or financial fraud, contact local authorities and the concerned banking institutions to alert them to the threat.

Evaluating Legitimacy of Investment Offers and Practicing Safe Online Transactions

By learning to evaluate opportunities and practice safe online financial habits, you can protect your hard-earned money. Let's explore vital strategies to recognize potential pitfalls and safeguard your finances.

The promise of quick and excessive gains often signals fraudulent schemes. It's essential to differentiate between realistic investment earnings and those that sound too good to be true. Genuine investments come with risks. You should understand these risk levels so you can make more informed decisions, ensuring you're not swayed by deceptive guarantees. Research plays a pivotal role in verifying the legitimacy of any financial opportunity. Before making commitments, vet the social media handles, businesses, and individuals offering ways to make money.

Consider the "Chase Glitch," a viral TikTok "get rich quick plan" that took flight over the 2024 Labor Day weekend faster than Frank Abagnale Jr did in real life. A modern-day version of the check cashing scheme featured video after video claiming that the glitch was a guaranteed way to get free money from Chase Bank. Many lined up with self-written checks outside of various Chase ATMs eagerly awaiting their turn—some even uploading videos of their accounts after the checks cleared. Most participants wrote themselves large checks (a few later uploaded videos showing their abject horror and dismay) when their accounts were frozen with colossal negative balances. Ouch, right? The Chase Glitch shows how quickly "fake news" travels in our digital age.

Also, it highlights the dire importance of verifying information directly from official sources before following a social media trend. Remember, legitimate financial institutions are bound to tell you that "restrictions apply," and they encourage you to check out their terms and conditions.

Our next notable entry was a crypto investment scam that fattened its victims up before taking them out to the slaughter. Scammers using dating apps or lurking on social media gradually built pseudo-relationships with their victims. Once the scammers built trust, they introduced the idea of investing in cryptocurrency. What made this scam dangerous was its long-term approach via social engineering tactics. Grooming took weeks or months before the topic of crypto (or money) was brought up, making it difficult to spot the red flags the scammers laid out. Victims have lost billions of dollars to this scam in the last couple of years alone.

One more example worth studying is the "Savings Challenge" scam that appeared on social media early in 2024. This third example promised that people could save $10,000 in about five months by following a special savings plan. And the catch was, users "just had to buy" a savings tracker via a paid subscription to access the "formula to success."

Consulting reliable sources like government websites or financial advisors can provide insights into whether an investment seems credible. For example, the U.S. Securities and Exchange Commission (SEC) offers resources to help avoid fraud. Check if others have had experiences with similar offers by searching terms like 'review,' 'scam,' or 'fraud' alongside the company's name. These steps can reveal red flags that might not be immediately obvious (Miller, 2024). Secure payment methods are also cornerstones of safe financial practices. Digital wallets and secure transaction apps provide an additional layer of protection when conducting online transactions.

These tools encrypt your financial details, reducing the possibility of unauthorized access. Choose platforms known for robust security measures, and enable features like two-factor authentication wherever possible. Monitoring your accounts regularly is key to catching unauthorized activities early. By keeping track of your transactions and balances, you can quickly spot discrepancies and unusual activities. Immediate action in response to these irregularities can prevent further unauthorized access. By setting up alerts for transactions over a specific amount, you can be notified immediately of any potential problems.

Staying updated on the latest scam trends is also beneficial. As technology evolves, so do methods used by scammers. Keeping yourself informed about new schemes helps you remain vigilant. Various financial watchdog agencies release regular updates on emerging scam tactics. Subscribing to their newsletters or following their social media handles can keep you abreast of developments in the financial fraud landscape (Get Smart About Money, 2017).

While navigating investment opportunities and financial safety, it's equally important to consult trusted friends or family members. Discussing potential investments with someone more experienced can provide a fresh perspective and highlight potential red flags. Often, those close to you can evaluate the situation objectively, providing valuable advice that might save you from costly mistakes.

Time constraints often imposed by scammers should raise suspicion. High-pressure sales tactics that push for immediate decisions typically aim to bypass thorough evaluation. Legitimate investments rarely demand rushed commitments. Understanding every aspect of the opportunity and seeking external validation can offer a safer path toward decision-making (Miller, 2024). Finally, remember the fundamental principle of skepticism.

Even amidst excitement, approach each new opportunity with caution. If anything feels off, trust your intuition and take a step back to reassess. It's better to miss one potential deal than to fall victim to a scam.

The Sum of Our Parts: Key Takeaways

We've now equipped you with essential skills to recognize and avoid financial scams in the digital age, where cyber threats are prevalent. It begins by examining common scams, from phishing attempts to fraudulent investment offers, emphasizing that scams often use enticing promises to lure individuals into financial traps. Through practical examples, you learned to identify red flags, such as poor grammar, suspicious email addresses, and unrealistic returns on investments, which often indicate deceptive intent.

You've been given actionable strategies, including checking sender details in emails, verifying URLs before clicking, and using two-factor authentication to secure online accounts. Real-life scenarios, like Ava's encounter with a fake influencer and William's experience with a phishing scheme on LinkedIn, illustrate the importance of skepticism and careful evaluation of online interactions.

In addition to identifying scams, I encourage you to consult trusted sources like the U.S. Securities and Exchange Commission (SEC) or financial advisors before making investment decisions. I want to emphasize the importance of monitoring your personal accounts for unusual activity and staying informed on evolving scam tactics. By fostering caution, vigilance, and awareness, you can navigate financial independence with confidence, making informed decisions while safeguarding your assets in an increasingly digital world.

Chapter 7:

Leveraging Technology for Financial Growth

As part of today's tech-savvy generation, you're discovering that you can harness technology to not only to simplify everyday transactions but also to pave a path toward a secure financial future. You have the power to manage your money effectively, set clear financial goals, and watch as you make progress—all with just a few taps on your smartphone. In this chapter, you'll find useful information about different finance apps and tools that are making a big difference.

We'll explore the benefits of budgeting apps that sync with your bank accounts, providing instant insights into your spending habits and helping you adjust them for better outcomes. Investment tools will be another focus, as these tools have made it easier than ever for those who are new to keeping track of their financial decisions. We'll discuss the importance of comparing these financial tools based on features, costs, and user experiences to ensure the best fit for your personal needs. Additionally, we'll address key security considerations when using these applications, making sure your sensitive information stays safe. The goal is to equip you with the knowledge needed to leverage technology for your financial growth and well-being.

Analyzing Finance Apps and Tools

Managing finances can seem like a daunting task. However, technology has revolutionized this aspect of life by offering various applications that simplify personal finance management. These tools enhance efficiency and clarity, helping individuals maintain control over their financial health effortlessly.

Budgeting apps are a game-changer for personal finance. These applications sync with bank accounts to provide real-time tracking of expenses, allowing users to see an accurate picture of their financial standing. Imagine waking up in the morning and, with one glance at your phone, knowing exactly how much you spent yesterday and what you have left in your monthly budget. This instant insight helps users make more informed decisions about their spending habits and adjust accordingly. Apps like Mint and YNAB categorize expenditures automatically, providing visual dashboards that highlight whether you're overspending or staying within limits.

Such features empower users to take immediate action to improve their financial health. On the investment front, technology has obliterated the traditional barriers that once made it challenging for beginners to enter the investing world. Today's investment tools feature user-friendly interfaces and educational resources that simplify complex financial concepts, rendering them accessible to those lacking a finance background. Robinhood, for instance, allows users to trade stocks with minimal effort via their smartphones, accompanying its trading functionalities with logical explanations of technical terms and strategies. Acorns has taken innovation a step further by rounding up spare change from everyday purchases and investing it automatically, thus integrating investment seamlessly into daily life. By reducing these obstacles, such tools cultivate a more inclusive investing environment and encourage young adults to accumulate wealth early.

Let's examine the experiences of Alyssa, a college student who had never considered investing until 2021. Like many of her peers, Alyssa was overwhelmed by the prospect of navigating the stock market, fearing that the complexity and jargon associated with investing would leave her frustrated and confused. However, when she discovered Robinhood during her sophomore year, everything changed. Intrigued by its simplicity and the promise of zero-commission trades, Alyssa downloaded the app and began her investment journey.

With the user-friendly interface guiding her, Alyssa quickly learned the fundamentals of buying and selling stocks. The educational resources within the app, including explanations of market trends and investment strategies, provided her with the knowledge she needed to feel confident in her decisions. She started by investing small amounts, experimenting with companies she was passionate about, such as tech startups and sustainable brands. As she gained experience, Alyssa diversified her portfolio, applying the lessons she had learned from the app's resources. Acorns, too, played a significant role in shaping Alyssa's investing journey. Despite her initial hesitations about market volatility, she was drawn to Acorns' seamless approach to investment. By linking her bank account, the app automatically rounded up her purchases, investing the spare change into diversified portfolios. This "set it and forget it" approach helped demystify investing further, allowing her to grow her wealth without the pressure of daily market monitoring.

Over the course of a year, Alyssa's investments in both platforms flourished, not only enhancing her financial literacy but also instilling a sense of empowerment. She began sharing her experience with classmates, encouraging them to explore these platforms. The community of young investors grew on campus, thanks to informal gatherings to discuss their successes, failures, and strategies. Alyssa's story reflects a larger trend as a study by The Motley Fool shows that many young investors embark on their financial journeys using platforms like Robinhood because of their user-friendly design and zero-commission trades (Caporal, 2023).

Technology has transformed the landscape of investing, with platforms like Robinhood and Acorns dismantling traditional barriers and offering significant benefits for financial health. As technology continues to make investment opportunities more accessible, you can (like Alyssa) harness the power of compound interest early on. By investing at a young age, she positioned herself to reap the benefits of long-term growth, planting the seeds for financial independence, retirement, and wealth accumulation. Embrace investing as an integral part of your financial life. This shift not only enhances your individual experience but also fosters a broader community of informed, engaged investors. Compare various financial tools to select the best strategy that suits your individual needs. Consider unique features, operating costs, and user experiences of these apps before committing to one. For instance, while both Mint and PocketGuard offer budgeting features, PocketGuard might better suit you if you want a quick snapshot of how much money is safe to spend after accounting for bills, goals, and necessities. Keep in mind that, while some apps are free, others might require subscription fees for unlocking advanced features. Researching and comparing these aspects can help you avoid unnecessary expenses and optimize your financial tool kit. If you're interested in investment apps, choosing between a robo-advisor like Betterment—which offers automated portfolio management—and a DIY trading app like E*TRADE can significantly influence your investing journey.

With the convenience of these technologies comes the need for you to understand security considerations. Personal finance apps handle sensitive information, including bank account details and social security numbers, which could be vulnerable if not properly secured. Ensure that the apps you choose prioritize topnotch security measures to protect your data. Most reputable financial apps use encryption technology to safeguard user data, but not every app implements the same level of protection. It's advisable to look for applications that offer two-factor authentication, regular software updates, and transparent privacy policies. Educating yourself on these security aspects ensures that your financial data stays protected from potential threats. Keeping abreast of recent reviews and expert opinions about app security can aid you in making safer choices.

Engaging With Online Finance Communities

Online communities have become a cornerstone for fostering your financial growth and collaboration, particularly through exposure to new strategies and shared experiences. By participating actively in finance forums or social media groups, you can uncover many benefits that significantly enhance your financial journey. Many people face similar financial challenges, whether it's managing debt, saving for a big purchase, or investing wisely. By connecting with others online, you can see just how common these struggles are; in turn, this helps to normalize such experiences and to reduce feelings of isolation. For example, if you're a college student worried about student loans, you might find solace when you browse through a forum and read about someone else's success story in paying off theirs. Such interactions not only offer emotional support but also present actionable advice from those who have been there before.

However, it's important to identify reputable online communities. The internet is vast, and not every group promotes genuine education and support. Look for communities that prioritize learning and sharing over product promotion. A good group will have members sharing insights into budgeting, investing, or savings without pushing specific products. For instance, a community focused on mutual learning might feature discussions about low-cost investment options, sustainable financial practices, or innovative savings methods, all providing fresh perspectives for you.

Now, let's talk about accountability partnerships. Interacting with peers who are on similar financial paths creates an environment where your motivation can flourish. When you share your financial goals within these communities, you're more likely to stay committed because there's a collective effort involved. Imagine setting a goal to save a particular amount by the end of the year and having a group of peers checking in on each other's progress. These accountability systems can be incredibly motivating for you. Aside from motivation, these communities serve as incredible networking platforms. You can connect with professionals across various financial sectors, opening doors for career advancement and mentorship opportunities. Engaging in thoughtful discussions or attending virtual events hosted by these communities can lead to valuable professional relationships. Imagine taking a keen interest in investment banking and engaging with seasoned professionals who provide insights, share industry secrets, and sometimes even offer internship opportunities. Networking fosters mentorship, which is invaluable for your career development. Experienced professionals can guide you as you navigate your way through your financial journey. They might offer advice on negotiating salary packages, understanding market trends, or making informed investment decisions. The beauty of such mentorship lies in its informality. It happens naturally through dialogues rather than structured programs, allowing for organic learning and relationship building for you.

Creating accountability partnerships requires some strategy on your part. Start by seeking active participants when you join a new community. Engage regularly in discussions to build rapport. Once comfortable, propose an accountability partnership with one or two other members who share similar goals as you. This can be as simple as checking in biweekly to discuss progress and challenges faced.

Being part of any community means giving as much as you take. Share your knowledge and experiences openly. If something worked well for you, explain why and how it might help others. Being genuine and approachable garners respect and encourages more open dialogue. Such contributions enrich the community, making it a more dynamic space for everyone involved, including you. Setting clear guidelines with your accountability partners can make a big difference in maintaining effective partnerships. Agreeing on regular check-ins, preferred communication methods, and ways to celebrate wins ensures that you all remain engaged. Such structures give room for conversations to flow freely while staying focused on the objectives at hand.

The Sum of Our Parts: Key Takeaways

Wrapping up this chapter, we learned how technology can be harnessed to simplify and strengthen your financial management efforts. By using budgeting and investment apps, such as Mint and YNAB, you gain insight into your spending habits and are empowered to make informed decisions. Apps like Robinhood and Acorns remove traditional barriers to investing, making it accessible even to those with minimal financial knowledge. Through examples like Alyssa's journey, we illustrate how these tools can transform financial literacy and build confidence in managing investments.

Choosing the right financial tools requires comparing features, costs, and security protocols. For example, some apps offer specific benefits, like PocketGuard's focus on tracking disposable income, while others, like Betterment, provide robo-advisory services for hands-off investing. I want to emphasize the importance of securing your personal information, and I strongly advise you to seek apps with two-factor authentication and robust encryption.

Engagement in online financial communities is also highlighted as a way to expand knowledge, gain support, and establish accountability partnerships. By connecting with peers and professionals, you can find motivation, receive guidance, and learn through shared experiences. With these tools and networks, you are equipped to take control of your finances, working toward stability and financial growth.

Chapter 8:

Cultivating a Mindset of Financial Empowerment

Cultivating a mindset of financial empowerment is essential for taking control of your financial future. This chapter invites you to embrace the power of self-discipline as a guiding force in achieving financial security. By adopting practices that foster delayed gratification and mindful spending, you're not only setting yourself up for success but also empowering yourself to make informed choices confidently. Imagine having the ability to resist impulsive purchases in favor of long-term stability; this skill doesn't just come naturally, but with practice, it's entirely attainable. The journey towards financial empowerment begins with small, deliberate steps that can transform into lifelong habits. We'll explore various strategies to strengthen your self-discipline in financial matters, and you'll learn the significance of establishing effective routines that seamlessly integrate into your daily life, reducing the likelihood of impulsive decisions. We'll delve into overcoming personal obstacles by identifying triggers that lead to reckless spending and developing resilience strategies to counteract them. Creating accountability systems will also be a focal point, providing you with tools to set and track financial goals, thus ensuring you're continually progressing towards your objectives. Additionally, we'll discuss how celebrating milestones along your journey reinforces positive behavior, keeping you motivated and on track. By the end of this chapter, you'll have a comprehensive tool kit for cultivating a mindset of financial empowerment. This tool kit will put you in prime position to navigate financial challenges with confidence and independence.

Developing Self-Discipline in Financial Matters

Self-discipline makes it easier for you to attain financial objectives and make informed decisions, particularly for young adults striving for financial autonomy. Recognizing how managing spending habits profoundly influences one's financial health is vital. Cultivating self-discipline entails mastering the concept of delaying gratification, forming productive routines, navigating personal challenges, and establishing systems of accountability. To illustrate this, consider Ingrid's story, which is a quest for financial independence after graduating from college.

With student loans looming over her, Ingrid realized that her spending habits directly affected her ability to save and invest. Instead of succumbing to immediate gratification, she made the conscious decision to prioritize her financial goals. Ingrid began by setting clear, actionable objectives. She mapped out her monthly budget, distinguishing between essential expenses and discretionary spending. This transparency allowed her to allocate funds prudently, ensuring she could meet her loan payments while also setting aside money for emergencies and future investments. Developing effective routines was another critical step in Ingrid's journey. She designated specific days for evaluating her financial situation, reviewing expenses, and adjusting her budget as necessary. This regular check-in became a cornerstone of her financial discipline, enabling her to stay on track and maintain a focus on her long-term goals. Ingrid also faced personal obstacles, including peer pressure when friends suggested spontaneous outings that could disrupt her budget.

Instead of giving in, she learned to communicate her financial goals with her friends, who ultimately respected her commitment to financial responsibility. By surrounding herself with supportive individuals, Ingrid strengthened her resolve, making it easier to resist temptations that could derail her progress. Accountability systems became a pivotal part of her strategy. Ingrid sought the support of a financial mentor, someone experienced who could provide guidance and share insights based on real-world experiences. This mentorship not only offered practical advice but also served as a reminder of her commitment to her financial objectives.

Because of her disciplined approach, Ingrid achieved remarkable progress. Within two years, she paid off her student loans and started investing in a retirement account. Her financial literacy improved significantly, allowing her to understand investment options better and make informed decisions about her future. Ingrid's case illustrates the profound impact of self-discipline on financial success.

By mastering her spending habits and creating structured routines, she transformed her financial landscape. For young adults seeking financial independence, the message is simple: Self-discipline is not merely a skill but a pathway to achieving lasting financial stability and growth.

Building Resilience and Stopping Impulsive Decisions

The idea of delayed gratification is an important element of any strategy related to long-term financial health. Delayed gratification means resisting the temptation to make short-term impulsive purchases in favor of saving for long-term benefits. Imagine you have a choice between buying that trendy gadget now or saving up for something more substantial like an emergency fund or your education. Choosing the latter can significantly contribute to financial stability. This mindset does not come naturally to everyone as it requires practice.

One method to cultivate this mindset is to set clear financial goals that are personally meaningful. For example, if owning a home is a dream, visualizing this goal can motivate you to save diligently instead of spending on short-lived pleasures. Tracking progress towards these goals can reinforce the importance of delaying gratification. Apps and journals can be effective in providing a visual reminder of how each small step contributes to the bigger picture.

Establishing financial routines is another component of good financial discipline. When we develop consistent habits regarding our finances, such as regular savings deposits or budgeting reviews, we reduce the likelihood of making impulsive purchases.

Consider setting a weekly budget session for yourself—perhaps every Sunday evening—to review expenses from the past week and plan for the next. This routine becomes a nonnegotiable part of your life, leading to better management of your finances. Guidelines for effective routines include automating savings where possible, which removes the temptation to spend money before it gets saved. Another strategy could involve categorizing expenses into needs and wants, allowing for more mindful spending decisions. By consistently adhering to such structured habits, you build a rhythm that gradually strengthens your financial resilience.

Overcoming obstacles to financial discipline requires identifying personal triggers and employing resilience strategies. Recognizing the situations or emotions that prompt you to spend recklessly is a significant first step. For some, stress shopping is a common trigger; for others, it's peer pressure. Once these triggers are identified, creating coping mechanisms—such as engaging in alternative activities like exercise or hobbies when the urge to spend arises—can be beneficial. Consider setbacks as learning opportunities, and adjust your approach accordingly. Seeking support through communities or mentors who share similar financial goals can offer encouragement and shared experiences, which further fortifies your resolve.

Creating accountability systems is another effective strategy for maintaining financial discipline. Sharing your financial goals with trusted friends or family members can increase your motivation to stay on track. When you know someone else is aware of your objectives, there is an added layer of commitment to uphold them. Using technology, such as financial apps, can aid in tracking commitments and celebrating milestones. These tools allow you to set reminders and visualize your progress, which can be both encouraging and rewarding. Establishing checkpoints—dates by which certain financial targets should be met—can create a structured path towards achieving your goals. These checkpoints provide tangible indicators of success and offer opportunities to adjust your plans if necessary. Also, celebrate small wins on your financial journey. Each goal you reach, even if it's small, is worth recognizing. This encouragement boosts your spirits and helps you stay committed to self-discipline.

Encouraging Bold Financial Learning and Growth

In a world where financial literacy isn't taught universally in schools, fostering a continuous desire for financial education becomes a must-have quality for you. As you step into higher education or the professional workforce, you often find yourself at a crossroads, making key financial decisions that can significantly affect your future. By embracing a mindset geared towards continuous learning, you empower yourself to make informed choices confidently.

Exploring diverse financial resources like books, podcasts, and workshops is an excellent start for you. These resources offer a wealth of knowledge from various perspectives, giving you insights into managing finances effectively. Financial books, ranging from practical guides to case studies, provide foundational knowledge and deep dives into topics like investing or budgeting. Podcasts bring expert voices directly to your ears, often breaking down complex concepts into simple, digestible discussions. Workshops and online courses offer interactive learning experiences, allowing for real-time questions and dynamic engagement. Each resource adds layers to your understanding, reinforcing the importance of lifelong learning in finance. Mistakes, though sometimes disheartening for you, are powerful teachers.

Financial missteps, whether it's overspending, accruing unnecessary debt, or poor investment choices, can transform into invaluable lessons for you. Reflecting on these errors helps you understand the consequences of your decisions, enabling you to adjust strategies and develop better habits. This mindset shift is essential; it leads to resilience and adaptability in the face of financial challenges. By analyzing past mistakes and learning from them, you build a solid foundation for making smarter choices in the future.

Through mentorship, you can discover insights and advice that are suitable to your financial situation. Engaging with financial mentors offers a personalized approach to navigating financial complexities. Mentors bring experience and perspective, guiding you through personal finance intricacies while offering practical solutions to specific problems. They serve as accountability partners, ensuring you stay on track with your financial goals. Mentorship also provides a safe space to discuss uncertainties and explore new opportunities without fear of judgment. This relationship fosters growth, confidence, and clarity, equipping you with the tools needed for financial success.

I cannot overstate the importance of sharing knowledge. When you share what you've learned about finance with friends, family, and peers, it not only reinforces your understanding but also cultivates a community dedicated to financial growth. This exchange of information creates a ripple effect, encouraging others to embark on their own learning journeys. As more people become financially literate, a generational shift occurs, enhancing overall financial well-being within communities. Sharing knowledge promotes inclusivity, ensuring that everyone has access to essential financial skills and insights necessary for navigating life's financial landscape. When you commit to financial education, you can reap numerous benefits. It reduces financial stress, improves decision-making capabilities, and empowers you to pursue your dreams confidently.

Financially literate individuals are more likely to plan for long-term goals, such as home ownership or retirement, and are less likely to fall into debilitating debt cycles. This education lays the groundwork for achieving financial independence and security, enabling you to break free from living paycheck to paycheck.

Your parents and educators can help you sustain your passion for financial education. Having open discussions with your parents about money management and learning from their experiences can help build your confidence to address present and future financial challenges. Teachers can also help you become even better prepared by providing you with resources, and by ideally integrating financial literacy into their curriculum. Don't be afraid to seek the wisdom of these mentor figures; your curiosity about financial matters will allow you to gain perspectives from your parents, your educators, and other individuals with relevant experience.

Creating systems to revisit and update your financial goals regularly ensures you remain aligned with your objectives. This practice encourages ongoing assessment of your financial strategies and fosters adaptability to changing circumstances.

Developing this routine cultivates consistency, reducing impulsive spending and promoting systematic savings.

The Sum of Our Parts: Key Takeaways

You are now armed with the mindset of financial empowerment, focusing on self-discipline, resilience, and continuous financial education. Developing self-discipline allows you to manage spending and prioritize long-term financial stability over impulsive purchases. Through examples like Ingrid's journey, we've illustrated how setting clear goals, establishing routines, and facing personal spending triggers can pave the way to financial independence. Embracing strategies such as delayed gratification and creating accountability systems helps reinforce these habits. We've also highlighted the importance of consistent learning in finance. By engaging with books, podcasts, and workshops, you can stay informed and adaptable, enabling you to make confident financial choices. Mentorship plays a key role, offering guidance tailored to your individual financial goals, while mistakes serve as valuable lessons that strengthen your resilience.

Finally, sharing financial knowledge fosters a community of informed individuals, supporting collective growth in financial literacy. Through continuous learning, regular goal assessments, and disciplined spending, you can navigate your financial journey with confidence and purpose, transforming challenges into opportunities for lasting financial security.

Keeping the Momentum Going

Now that you've got the tools to take charge of your financial journey, it's time to share your newfound knowledge with others who are also searching for guidance.

By leaving your honest opinion of *Money Smarts* on Amazon, you'll be helping other young adults who want to make confident money decisions find the resource they need. Your review could be the reason someone feels empowered to take the next step in their financial journey.

Thank you for being part of this mission. Financial wisdom grows stronger when we share what we've learned—and you're helping me do just that.

Scan the QR code to leave your review on Amazon.

Conclusion

In conclusion, we've taken you on a journey through the critical steps of financial empowerment, guiding you from the basics of budgeting to the more complex areas of saving, investing, and building wealth. By understanding the different sources of income, distinguishing between needs and wants, and developing a mindful approach to spending, you've set a strong foundation for financial stability. Each chapter was crafted to provide you with a comprehensive toolkit, whether you're navigating your first job, managing debt, or planning for significant future investments. The lessons on setting clear goals, maintaining financial discipline, and cultivating resilience are invaluable, encouraging you to make sound financial decisions that reflect your personal values and aspirations.

This journey toward financial independence is ongoing, requiring continued learning, adapting, and refining of your approach. As life changes, so too will your financial needs and priorities, and it's essential to revisit and update your financial strategies regularly. Embrace these changes as opportunities for growth, knowing that each decision made today contributes to long-term financial health.

Remember, financial success is not about perfection but about persistence and the willingness to keep improving. Let this book be a reference as you move forward, drawing upon the principles and practices shared here whenever you need guidance or motivation. Finally, celebrate each milestone you achieve along the way. Financial empowerment is both a journey and a reward, providing peace of mind and freedom. You now possess the knowledge and tools to create a future of security and opportunity.

As you continue on this path, remember the words of Eleanor Roosevelt: "The future belongs to those who believe in the beauty of their dreams."

Here's to building a financially resilient future and the dreams it enables.

References

7 steps for how to spot email phishing. (2023, June 6). Cofense.com. https://cofense.com/knowledge-center/how-to-spot-phishing

Achieving your goals: The essential role of self discipline. (2023, October 8). 7goodminutes.com. https://7goodminutes.com/achieving-your-goals-the-essential-role-of-self-discipline/

Al. (2015, March 1). *Personal finance software solutions: Mint vs. personal capital.* Saving the Crumbs. https://savingthecrumbs.com/mint-vs-personal-capital/

Alliant Credit Union. (2024, August 13). *Increase your emergency fund with a High-Yield savings account: How much you should save.* Alliant Credit Union. https://www.alliantcreditunion.org/money-mentor/high-yield-savings-account-for-emergency-fund-how-much-should-you-save

Ayoola, E., & Tindall, T. (2024, October 16). *28 proven ways to save money.* NerdWallet.

https://www.nerdwallet.com/article/finance/how-to-save-money

Bach, D. (2016, December 27). *The automatic millionaire, expanded and updated: A powerful one-step plan to live and finish rich.* Crown Currency.

Banus, S. (n.d.). *Personal Capital vs. Mint – Which should you use?* Stepwise. https://stepwisewealth.com/review/personal-capital-vs-mint/

Bennett, K. (2024, July 1). *What's the difference between fixed and variable expenses?* Bankrate. https://www.bankrate.com/banking/fixed-expenses-vs-variable-expenses/

Bennett, R. (2024, September 30). *Short-term vs. long-term goals: Best savings strategies to use for each.* Bankrate. https://www.bankrate.com/banking/savings/strategies-for-short-and-long-term-financial-goals/

Berger, R. (2023, January 11). *Personal capital (Empower) vs mint: My ratings after using both for years.* RobBerger.com. https://robberger.com/personal-capital-vs-mint/

Bouchrika, I. (2024, October 29). *Building financial literacy: Empowering students to invest in stocks.* Research.com. https://research.com/education/building-financial-literacy-empowering-students-to-invest-in-stocks

Burnette, M. (2024, February 8). *Emergency fund: What it is and why it matters.* NerdWallet.

https://www.nerdwallet.com/article/banking/emergen
cy-fund-why-it-matters

Caporal, J. (2023, November 27). *Gen Z and millennial investors: Ranking the most used, trusted investing tools.* https://www.fool.com/research/gen-z-millennial-investors-tools/

Carr, L. (2024, August 27). *30 remote side hustles that you can do from anywhere.* Whop. https://whop.com/blog/remote-side-hustles/

Chen, J. (2024, April 16). *Investing: An introduction.* Investopedia. https://www.investopedia.com/articles/basics/11/3-s-simple-investing.asp

Cope, S. (2024, September 17). *18 effective time management strategies and techniques.* Upwork. https://www.upwork.com/resources/time-management-strategies

Coursera. (2023, June 16). *6 time management tips to boost your productivity.* https://www.coursera.org/ca/articles/time-management

Craggs, R. (2024, February 22). *What are the benefits of revenue diversification?* The Bottom Line.

https://mercury.com/blog/revenue-diversification-benefits

Credit cards. (n.d.). Federal Trade Commission. https://www.ftc.gov/news-events/topics/consumer-finance/credit-cards

DeNicola, L. (2024, April 10). *How to establish credit as a young person.* Experian. https://www.experian.com/blogs/ask-experian/how-to-establish-credit-as-a-young-person/

Eight common investment scams and how to spot them. (2024, February 21). GetSmarterAboutMoney.ca. https://www.getsmarteraboutmoney.ca/learning-path/types-of-fraud/8-common-investment-scams/

Fixed vs. variable expenses. (2024, September 9). MetLife. https://www.metlife.com/stories/personal-finance/fixed-vs-variable-costs/

Fontinelle, A. (2024, February 25). *How to set financial goals for your future.* Investopedia. https://www.investopedia.com/articles/personal-finance/100516/setting-financial-goals/

Ganti, A. (2024, May 17). *What is a budget? Plus 11 budgeting myths holding you back.* Investopedia. https://www.investopedia.com/terms/b/budget.asp

Houston, M. (2024, April 17). *Why diversifying your income streams is essential in today's economy.* Forbes. https://www.forbes.com/sites/melissahouston/2024/

04/17/why-diversifying-your-income-streams-is-essential-in-todays-economy/

How to avoid fraud. (n.d.). Investor.gov. https://www.investor.gov/protect-your-investments/fraud/how-avoid-fraud

Jacobs Strategy. (2022, March). *Boldly moving forward.* https://s29.q4cdn.com/159670324/files/doc_presentation/2022/03/Jacobs-2022-2024-Strategy-_-Boldly-Moving-Forward.pdf

Learn about the importance of financial literacy month with members of our finance and accounting teams. (2022, May 2). Cengage Group. https://www.cengagegroup.com/news/perspectives/2022/learn-about-the-importance-of-financial-literacy-month-with-members-of-our-finance-and-accounting-teams/

M1 Team. (2024, September 10). *Creating a value-based budget: Aligning your spending with personal priorities.* M1. https://m1.com/knowledge-bank/creating-a-value-based-budget-aligning-your-spending-with-personal-priorities/

Making a budget. (n.d.). Consumer.gov. https://consumer.gov/managing-your-money/making-budget

Managing investment risk: 3 factors that can help reduce investment risk. (n.d.). Ameriprise Financial. https://www.ameriprise.com/financial-goals-priorities/investing/strategies-to-help-reduce-investment-risk

Mark, M., & McKay, J. (2015, January 1). *Are traditional benefits good enough?* Benefits Canada. https://www.benefitscanada.com/benefits/health-benefits/are-traditional-benefits-good-enough/

Martinez, Z. (2024, June 7). *The ultimate guide to finance networking events.* Paystand. https://www.paystand.com/blog/finance-networking-events

Mastering your schedule: Effective time management strategies for success. (2024, May 9). Penn LPS Online. https://lpsonline.sas.upenn.edu/features/mastering-your-schedule-effective-time-management-strategies-success

McMullen, L., & Ayoola, E. (2024, October 15). *The best budget apps for 2024.* NerdWallet. https://www.nerdwallet.com/article/finance/best-budget-apps

Miller, T. (2024, July 15). *Can you spot an investment scam?* Federal Trade Commission Consumer Advice.

https://consumer.ftc.gov/consumer-alerts/2024/07/can-you-spot-investment-scam

Murphy, R. (2024, October 28). *Best budgeting apps of November 2024.* https://www.forbes.com/advisor/banking/best-budgeting-apps/

Non-traditional versus traditional employee benefits. (n.d.). HRZone. https://hrzone.com/glossary/non-traditional-versus-traditional-employee-benefits/

Personal Capital vs. Mint vs. Kubera: Which one is best for you? (n.d.). Kubera.com. https://www.kubera.com/blog/personal-capital-vs-mint-vs-kubera

Picardo, E. (2024, July 19). *Investing explained: Types of investments and how to get started.* Investopedia. https://www.investopedia.com/terms/i/investing.asp

Porter, K. (2024, June 14). *Struggling with overspending? The envelope budgeting method.* Fortune Recommends. https://fortune.com/recommends/banking/envelope-budgeting-method/

Protect yourself from phishing. (n.d.). support.microsoft.com. https://support.microsoft.com/en-us/windows/protect-yourself-from-phishing-0c7ea947-ba98-3bd9-7184-430e1f860a44

Ritchie, N. (2024, August 21). *6 traditional and creative benefits to offer employees.* Iamagazine.com.

https://www.iamagazine.com/strategies/6-traditional-and-creative-benefits-to-offer-employees

Sam. (n.d.). *How does Personal Capital compare to Mint?* Financial Samurai. https://www.financialsamurai.com/how-does-personal-capital-compare-to-mint/

Schmitz, T. (2023, July 25). *Why mastering self-control is key for financial success.* The Conover Company. https://www.conovercompany.com/why-mastering-self-control-is-key-for-financial-success/

Schwahn, L. (2024, August 12). *What is a budget?* NerdWallet. https://www.nerdwallet.com/article/finance/what-is-a-budget

Sethi, R. (2009, March 23). *I will teach you to be a rich.* Workman Publishing.

Tamplin, T. (2024, March 13). *5 common budgeting methods that can build financial security.* Forbes. https://www.forbes.com/sites/truetamplin/2024/03/12/5-common-budgeting-methods-that-can-build-financial-security/

Top traditional versus non-traditional employee benefits. (2024, July 26). Smart Workforce. https://smartworkforce.co.uk/traditional-versus-non-traditional-employee-benefits/

Understand your credit score. (n.d.). Consumer Financial Protection Bureau.

https://files.consumerfinance.gov/f/documents/cfpb_adult-fin-ed_understand-your-credit-score.pdf

Verlinden, N. (n.d.). *Types of employee benefits: 17 benefits HR should know.* AIHR. https://www.aihr.com/blog/types-of-employee-benefits/

Walker, L. (2024, May 7). *The future of finance: Collaborative innovation at the crossroads of technology and tradition.* Fintech-tables.com. https://fintech-tables.com/the-power-of-collaboration/

Warren, E., & Tyagi, A. W. (2005). *All your worth: The ultimate lifetime money plan.* Simon & Schuster.

Ways to help reduce risk in your portfolio. (2022, March 13). Charles Schwab. https://www.schwab.com/learn/story/ways-to-help-reduce-risk-your-portfolio

What is budgeting? What is a budget? (n.d.). mymoneycoach.ca. https://www.mymoneycoach.ca/budgeting/what-is-a-budget-planning-forecasting

Willie KG. (2024, October 4). *23 side hustle jobs that pay good money each month.* Task Landing. https://tasklanding.com/side-hustle-jobs/

Yakal, K. (2024, October 14). *The best personal finance and budgeting apps for 2024.* PC Mag. https://www.pcmag.com/picks/the-best-personal-finance-services